Dividend Investing for Beginners

*A Simple, Succinct & Comprehensive Guide to Dividend
Investing for UK Investors*

William Pembroke

Table of Contents

Chapter 1: Introduction to Dividend Investing 1

Chapter 2: Understanding Dividends 5

Chapter 3: The Power of Compound Interest 9

Chapter 4: The UK Dividend Landscape 15

Chapter 5: The Taxation of Dividends in the UK 19

Chapter 6: Creating a Dividend Investing Plan 23

Chapter 7: Finding Dividend Stocks 28

Chapter 8: Dividend Aristocrats in the UK 34

Chapter 9: Dividend Reinvestment Plans (DRIPs) 38

Chapter 10: How to Analyse a Dividend Stock 43

Chapter 11: Avoiding Dividend Traps 48

Chapter 12: Building a Diversified Dividend Portfolio 54

Chapter 13: Investment Vehicles for Dividend Investing
.... 59

Chapter 14: Timing the Market vs Time in the Market 64

Chapter 15: Famous Dividend Investors and Their
Strategies 69

Chapter 16: Learning from Historic Dividend Crises .. 74

Chapter 17: Dividend Investing vs Capital Appreciation
.... 78

Chapter 18: Impact of Economic Cycles on Dividend
Investing 83

Chapter 19: Inflation and Dividend Investing 88

Chapter 20: Investing in International Dividends from
the UK 92

Chapter 21: The Role of Dividends in Retirement Planning 97

Chapter 22: Using Dividends for Passive Income 101

Chapter 23: Real Estate Investment Trusts (REITs) and Dividends 106

Chapter 24: Investing in Dividend Growth Stocks 112

Chapter 25: Monitoring and Rebalancing Your Dividend Portfolio 118

Chapter 26: Dividend Policy and Corporate Governance 123

Chapter 27: Ethical and Sustainable Dividend Investing 130

Chapter 28: Dividends vs Buybacks 136

Chapter 29: Advanced Dividend Concepts 142

Chapter 30: Conclusion - The Future of Dividend Investing in the UK 146

Our Thanks and A Request 152

CHAPTER 1:

Introduction to Dividend Investing

When we embark on the journey of investing, there are myriad paths to tread. Today, we begin our voyage on a route less exciting for some, yet one that holds the promise of consistent returns and relative safety – the path of dividend investing. By choosing to become dividend investors, we are favouring a method that puts faith in the power of reinvestment and the compounding of those reinvested dividends. This is an approach that is very much in tune with my own philosophy, for it recognises the importance of patient, long-term investing.

Let us start by defining what we mean by dividend investing. In its simplest form, when you purchase shares in a company, you become a part-owner of that business. As such, you are entitled to a share of the profits. Some companies, particularly those with established businesses and steady earnings, choose to distribute a portion of these profits to shareholders. These payments are known as dividends. The practice of buying shares in these companies, with an aim to generate regular income from the dividends, is what we refer to as dividend investing.

If you've just started to dip your toes into the investing waters, you might wonder why you should consider

1

dividend investing, particularly in the UK market. This book is here to guide you along this path, explaining its unique challenges and opportunities.

In the investment arena, dividends have traditionally been viewed as a sign of a company's health and stability. A company that has a consistent record of paying dividends is likely one that has reliable, steady earnings. This sends a positive signal to investors about the company's financial health. Furthermore, dividends are tangible, they represent real earnings, as opposed to potential future growth.

When we view dividend investing as part of a broader portfolio strategy, its importance becomes even clearer. In a balanced portfolio, dividend investing plays a crucial role. Dividends can provide a steady stream of income, making them particularly attractive to those seeking regular returns such as retirees. Furthermore, during periods of market volatility, dividends can offer a degree of stability. They can form a cushion that helps soften the blow of price fluctuations, providing regular returns even when share prices fall.

To understand the appeal of dividend investing within the context of the UK, we should take a brief look at its history and evolution in this market. The practice of paying dividends goes back hundreds of years, with the earliest joint-stock corporations offering a share of profits to their investors. In the UK, many companies have a long history of regular dividend payments, reflecting their mature and stable business operations.

Over the years, UK investors have seen both the highs and lows of dividend investing. The latter part of the 20th century saw strong dividend growth, as the economy expanded and businesses thrived. However, the dot-com crash of the early 2000s and the financial crisis of 2008 served as harsh reminders of the dangers of overexposure to a single investment style or sector. Despite these crises, many companies continued to pay dividends, further underlining their importance in a balanced portfolio.

In the UK, the tradition of dividends is deeply entrenched in the investment landscape. UK companies have generally exhibited a strong propensity to pay dividends, with many investors expecting and depending on this source of income. This cultural emphasis on dividends is one reason why dividend investing remains an attractive proposition for many UK investors. It's also why it's important for you, as a new investor, to understand this particular aspect of the market.

In conclusion, dividend investing offers a conservative, yet potentially rewarding path to investment success. It is a method that aligns with a philosophy of patience, stability, and long-term growth, traits that echo my own investment ethos. The journey we are embarking on will not be without its challenges. Yet, with careful navigation and an understanding of the basic principles that we will explore in this book, you too can unlock the potential of dividends and use them as an effective tool in your investment toolkit. As we turn to the chapters ahead, we'll delve deeper into understanding dividends, the power of compound interest, and the unique features of the UK dividend landscape. It's an exciting journey, and I'm glad you've chosen to embark on it.

CHAPTER 2:

Understanding Dividends

At the heart of dividend investing lies a simple yet powerful concept: dividends. In essence, dividends represent the portion of a company's earnings returned to shareholders. But what does that really mean? How does it work? And more importantly, how can it benefit you, the investor? These are the questions we aim to answer in this chapter, for understanding dividends is the first stepping stone in your journey of dividend investing.

To start at the beginning, a dividend is a sum of money paid regularly by a company to its shareholders from its profits. Companies generate earnings (profits) through their operations, and these earnings are either retained for future growth or returned to shareholders as dividends. In essence, when you hold shares in a company, you are part-owner of that business, and dividends are your share of the profits.

Importantly, not all companies pay dividends. Those that do are typically well-established firms with stable, predictable profits and a surplus of cash. Startups and growth companies, on the other hand, often reinvest all of their earnings back into the business, leaving no surplus for dividends. For these companies, the aim is to fuel growth and increase the company's value, rewarding investors with capital gains when the stock price appreciates.

The decision to pay dividends, and how much to pay, falls under the purview of a company's board of directors. They consider factors such as the company's profitability, future growth prospects, and industry norms before making a decision. This is why consistent dividend payment can be a sign of a financially healthy company with strong governance.

Now, you might be thinking, "That's all well and good, but how does a dividend translate into pounds and pence for me?" The answer lies in understanding different types of dividends and the related concepts of dividend yield and dividend payout ratio.

Types of Dividends

Broadly, dividends fall into two categories: regular dividends and special dividends. Regular dividends, as the name suggests, are paid out regularly, typically on a quarterly, semi-annual, or annual basis. These are the dividends that companies commit to and strive to maintain or gradually increase over time. Regular dividends are typically the focus of dividend investors because of their predictability and stability.

On the other hand, special dividends are one-off payments made by companies in addition to regular dividends. They often result from exceptional business circumstances like the sale of a subsidiary, a windfall gain, or an unusually profitable year. Special dividends can be a pleasant surprise for investors, but they are not consistent or predictable.

Dividend Yield and Dividend Payout Ratio

Dividend yield and dividend payout ratio are two essential tools for comparing the dividends of different companies. The dividend yield measures the return on investment from dividends alone, expressed as a percentage of the share price. It's calculated by dividing the annual dividends per share by the price per share. A higher yield indicates a larger return in terms of dividends.

However, a high yield isn't always a good thing. It could be the result of a falling share price rather than generous dividends. It could also indicate that the company is returning too much to shareholders and not reinvesting enough in future growth. This is why savvy investors consider the dividend yield in conjunction with the dividend payout ratio.

The dividend payout ratio is the proportion of earnings paid out as dividends. It's calculated by dividing the annual dividends per share by the earnings per share. This ratio gives insight into a company's dividend sustainability. A high payout ratio may suggest that a company is distributing most of its profits, leaving little for future investment or to buffer against future downturns. On the other hand, a low payout ratio may indicate room for future dividend growth.

The beauty of dividend investing lies in understanding and utilising these concepts to select companies that pay sustainable and growing dividends. These dividends can then be reinvested, used to supplement income, or even fund a retirement. But before we delve further into these aspects, we must appreciate the magic of compound interest, the engine that powers dividend investing, which we will explore in the next chapter.

CHAPTER 3:

The Power of Compound Interest

Our foray into the world of dividends wouldn't be complete without discussing an essential principle that shapes investment returns over the long term, irrespective of whether you're in Bristol or Boston. This principle is compound interest, often referred to as the 'eighth wonder of the world'.

Firstly, let us define compound interest. In its simplest form, compound interest refers to the process by which the interest you earn on an investment begins to earn interest itself. The initial sum of money grows at an exponential rate rather than a linear one because the interest is effectively 'compounded' over time.

To elucidate, consider a simple interest scenario. If you invest £1,000 at an annual interest rate of 5%, you would have £1,050 after one year and £1,100 after two years. You simply earn £50 each year because the interest is applied only to the original amount or the 'principal'. Contrastingly, under compound interest, that same £1,000 investment would grow to £1,050 after the first year, similar to the simple interest scenario. However, in the second year, you earn interest not only on your initial £1,000 but also on the £50 interest from the first year. This means you'll have £1,102.50 at the end of two years. It's a small difference at first glance, but it's in these seemingly

9

inconsequential details that the magic lies. The effects of compound interest become truly remarkable over extended periods.

In fact, Albert Einstein purportedly said, "Compound interest is the most powerful force in the universe." Although we cannot verify if he indeed made this statement, it certainly encompasses the truth. Compound interest is a potent tool for wealth creation, especially for investors who harness its power early and remain patient.

Dividends play a pivotal role in the compounding process. When you receive dividends and reinvest them, you're increasing the number of shares you own. Consequently, you receive even more dividends in the future, given that dividends are typically paid per share. Therefore, those dividends can then be used to purchase more shares, continuing the cycle and leading to a snowballing effect.

Consider a dividend-paying company whose share you've purchased for £100. If this company has a dividend yield of 5%, you would receive £5 as dividends at the end of the year. If you reinvest these dividends by purchasing more of the company's stock, you now have £105 worth of shares in the company. In the following year, assuming the dividend yield remains constant, you will receive £5.25 in dividends. The cycle of reinvesting dividends allows your investment to grow exponentially over time, provided you resist the temptation to cash out your dividends.

To further illustrate this point, let's observe an example from the UK market. Suppose an investor in the late 1980s decided to buy £1,000 worth of shares in a leading British company with a consistent track record of paying dividends. For simplicity's sake, let's say this company maintained an average annual dividend yield of 4%. Fast forward to today, over three decades later. Had our investor taken every dividend payout and spent it, their shareholdings in the company would still be worth £1,000. But suppose they chose to reinvest the dividends. In that case, they would now have a significantly larger number of shares due to the compounding effect, potentially worth tens of thousands of pounds, depending on the price appreciation of the shares.

Investing is not just about earning returns. It's about earning returns on your returns. Over an extended period, the effects of compound interest can significantly magnify your wealth. This point is worth stressing because compounding works best when given time. It's like planting a tree. You won't see much growth initially, but given enough time, you will see a tall tree that can provide shade and bear fruit.

However, a word of caution here: While compound interest is a powerful tool, it requires discipline and patience. It works quietly in the background, and the extraordinary effects take time to materialize. As such, it might seem like nothing is happening in the initial years, leading some to abandon their strategy prematurely. Yet, it is essential to remember that the most substantial growth occurs in the later years due to the exponential nature of compound interest. Therefore, it's important to stick to your strategy and let compounding work its magic.

Moreover, the principle of compounding is not merely numerical but philosophical as well. It emphasises consistency, patience, and long-term growth. It encourages you to focus on gradual, steady accumulation, rather than getting rich quick.

As a wise man once said, "The stock market is a device for transferring money from the impatient to the patient." This quote is widely attributed to Warren Buffett, although there is debate about its origin. Irrespective of who said it first, the quote certainly carries a nugget of wisdom, especially for dividend investors. In the world of investing, patience is not just a virtue but a route to wealth.

The potency of compound interest lies in its ability to grow wealth exponentially over time. But words alone might not fully capture its effect. Therefore, let's explore three specific examples that highlight the effect of compound interest over different timeframes and at different rates. For each of these examples, we will consider an investor who starts with an initial investment of £10,000 and reinvests all dividends received.

Example 1: 10 Years at 4% Interest

Consider an investor who starts with an initial investment of £10,000. Their portfolio includes dividend-paying stocks that yield a steady 4% per annum, with all dividends being reinvested. After ten years, due to the magic of compound interest, the original investment would have grown to about £14,802. This represents a 48% increase on the initial investment. The effect may seem modest, but the real power of compounding becomes more noticeable over longer periods.

Example 2: 20 Years at 7% Interest

Now, let's expand the timeframe to 20 years with a slightly higher annual return of 7%. Remarkably, the original investment of £10,000 would now have escalated to approximately £38,697. Despite only a 3% increase in the annual return, the end balance has more than doubled compared to the first example. This substantial increase attests to the astounding impact of compound interest, which amplifies over longer timeframes and at higher rates of return.

Example 3: 30 Years at 9% Interest

Finally, let's up the stakes further and examine an investment held for 30 years that yields an even higher annual return of 9%. In this scenario, the initial £10,000 investment would have mushroomed to an impressive £132,676. This is more than a thirteenfold increase on the initial investment, all thanks to the power of compounding.

These examples highlight the transformative power of compound interest: it rewards both patience and higher returns. Even small increases in the annual return, when compounded over extended periods, can result in substantially larger sums.

However, it's essential to remember that these examples somewhat simplify the complexities of real-world investing. They assume a consistent return year after year, which isn't usually the case with investments. Market fluctuations, changes in dividend policies, taxes, transaction costs, and other factors can all impact returns.

Still, the principle holds true: the power of compounding can significantly amplify your investment returns over the long run, particularly when you reinvest dividends. Despite the inevitable market ups and downs, the overall trend of the market has historically been upward. Therefore, patient investors who harness the power of compounding stand to reap the rewards. By consistently reinvesting dividends and allowing your investments to grow over time, you give your wealth the best opportunity to flourish.

The power of compounding is fundamental to understanding why dividends are such a critical component of total return and why a long-term perspective is necessary in dividend investing. Armed with this understanding, you're better equipped to appreciate why investing in dividend-paying companies can be such a profitable strategy. With compound interest on your side, you're not just working for your money; your money is working for you.

CHAPTER 4:

The UK Dividend Landscape

As we delve deeper into the world of dividend investing, it's paramount that we look closely at the environment from which we will be picking our dividend-paying companies. In this chapter, we are going to explore the UK dividend landscape.

The United Kingdom is renowned for its robust, diverse and well-regulated financial markets. Its status as a financial powerhouse is recognised globally, and it has a long-standing history of being a hub for investors seeking to grow their wealth. But within the broader realm of investment, one area that the UK particularly shines in is dividend investing.

The culture of dividends is deeply ingrained within the UK corporate ethos. Many UK-based companies pride themselves on maintaining, and where possible, increasing their dividends each year, providing a steady stream of income for their investors. This habit has turned the UK into one of the most reliable sources of dividends globally. A 2019 study by Janus Henderson showed that the UK accounted for 11.2% of all dividends paid worldwide, placing it second only to the United States.

UK companies typically distribute dividends biannually, once as an 'interim' dividend and then as a 'final' dividend.

The interim dividend is usually declared partway through the company's financial year and is generally smaller, while the final dividend comes after the year's financial results are known. This setup can lead to a steady stream of income throughout the year for investors.

Now, let's turn our attention to the historic data of UK dividend yields, which will provide us with useful insights into the performance and trends in the UK dividend landscape. According to a 2020 study by Barclays, the average dividend yield for the FTSE All-Share Index – which represents the performance of all eligible companies listed on the London Stock Exchange's main market – over the past decade has hovered around 3.5%. However, yields have varied between sectors, with more defensive sectors like Utilities and Consumer Goods typically offering higher yields than growth-oriented sectors like Technology and Consumer Services.

One noticeable trend in the UK dividend landscape is the high concentration of dividends amongst a small group of companies. Research has shown that the top 15 dividend-paying companies often account for around half of all dividends paid out in the UK. While this does demonstrate the robust commitment of these companies to return capital to their shareholders, it does underline the importance of diversification when building a dividend-focused portfolio, which we will explore in a later chapter.

However, as the financial market is always in flux, the dividend landscape in the UK has also faced its fair share of challenges. One of the more recent ones was the dividend cuts that occurred in the wake of the COVID-19 pandemic. Many UK companies, particularly in sectors most affected by lockdown measures such as Retail, Travel, and Leisure, were forced to cut or even suspend their dividends to conserve cash in the face of severe business disruption. According to a report by Link Group, UK dividends fell by 44% in 2020 as companies tried to protect their balance sheets from the economic fallout of the pandemic.

Yet, even amid such turbulence, many companies maintained their dividend payouts. Those with strong balance sheets and cash flows, as well as those in more defensive sectors, were able to continue rewarding their shareholders. This resilience underscores the importance of focusing on companies with robust fundamentals when choosing dividend stocks – another topic that we will cover in a later chapter.

The UK government's approach to corporate governance also plays a role in supporting a strong dividend culture. UK-listed companies are bound by the UK Corporate Governance Code, which places a strong emphasis on the rights of shareholders. Companies are encouraged to return surplus capital to shareholders, typically in the form of dividends, unless they can demonstrate that reinvesting within the business would provide better returns.

To conclude, the UK provides an attractive landscape for dividend investors, shaped by a corporate culture that values the return of capital to shareholders and strong regulatory standards. Its diverse economy offers a range of opportunities across various sectors, though a degree of caution is needed given the concentration of dividends amongst a small number of firms.

However, as we've noted, the landscape isn't static. Dividend investing in the UK, like anywhere else, comes with its challenges and risks. The unexpected can and does happen, as the recent pandemic illustrated all too clearly. But by understanding the landscape in which we are investing, we can better navigate these challenges and place ourselves in a position to reap the benefits that dividend investing has to offer.

In subsequent chapters, we'll build on this understanding of the UK dividend landscape, exploring how to find the right dividend stocks, manage risks, and ultimately construct a dividend-focused portfolio that aligns with your financial goals. By equipping ourselves with the right knowledge, tools, and strategies, we can harness the power of dividends to generate a steady stream of income and achieve long-term financial growth.

CHAPTER 5:

The Taxation of Dividends in the UK

Every dividend investor's journey will inevitably lead them to a crossroads, a point of intersection between the joy of earning dividends and the sober reality of taxes. The structure of the United Kingdom's taxation system for dividends isn't merely a footnote for UK investors but a fundamental part of the investing process. Knowledge of these tax structures and their influence on your returns is an indispensable piece of your investing puzzle. This chapter aims to explore this complex labyrinth, shedding light on the crucial elements of dividend taxation and guiding you towards more informed and effective investing decisions.

In the realm of dividend investing, understanding taxation begins with understanding the three tiers of the UK's tax rates on dividends: the basic rate, the higher rate, and the additional rate. These rates, however, are only applicable once your dividends exceed a specific threshold known as the Dividend Allowance.

The UK government has instituted the Dividend Allowance, a tax-free buffer on the first £2,000 of dividends you receive in a tax year. This allowance is not related to the rate at which you pay tax. Instead, it applies universally to all dividend investors, regardless of whether you pay tax at the basic rate, higher rate, or additional rate. This means that you pay zero tax on the first £2,000 of dividend income. After exceeding this threshold, the amount of tax you pay on your dividends will depend on the income tax band you fall into.

Dividends that transcend the Dividend Allowance are subjected to tax. At the basic rate, the tax stands at 7.5%. This is applicable if your overall taxable income, inclusive of dividends, is less than or equal to £50,270. Once your total income ascends into the higher rate tax bracket (between £50,271 and £150,000), your dividend tax increases to 32.5%. For the financially fortunate few whose total income exceeds £150,000, dividends are taxed at an additional rate of 38.1%.

Now, armed with the understanding of the UK dividend tax structure, let's venture into the process of dividend taxation. How does it work in practice? Well, dividends are paid out of profits on which the company has already paid or is due to pay Corporation Tax. Dividends received by shareholders are then deemed to have had a 10% tax credit deducted at source.

The implications of the aforementioned tax credits are no longer significant for individual shareholders, as the cost of the tax credit cannot be reclaimed, and the tax credit cannot be used to cover tax on other income. The only relevance is in calculating the tax you owe on your dividends.

One of the keys to minimising tax exposure is found in efficient use of tax wrappers. For many UK investors, Individual Savings Accounts (ISAs) and Self-Invested Personal Pensions (SIPPs) have proved to be two potent weapons in the tax-efficient investing arsenal.

ISAs serve as a tax shelter for investors. Any dividends received from investments held within an ISA are not subjected to further tax, regardless of your tax band. There is an annual allowance for contributions to an ISA, currently capped at £20,000 per tax year. This facility enables the growth and dividend income within the ISA to be shielded from tax, providing a significant advantage, particularly for higher and additional rate taxpayers.

A SIPP, meanwhile, functions as a type of pension investment that affords investors tax relief on contributions. The tax relief equates to a refund at your marginal rate of tax. This means that if you are a basic rate taxpayer, for every £80 you contribute to your SIPP, the government tops this up to £100. Higher and additional rate taxpayers can claim back even more through their self-assessment tax return. Like the ISA, investments within a SIPP grow free from capital gains tax, and dividends are not subjected to further tax.

These tax wrappers can be part of a strategy to reduce or, in some cases, avoid dividend tax. However, they do come with restrictions. ISAs, while offering greater flexibility on withdrawals, limit your annual contributions. SIPPs, on the other hand, offer higher annual contribution limits but are less flexible on withdrawals, tying your investments until you reach the minimum pension age (currently 55, but rising to 57 by 2028).

Another consideration in the quest for tax efficiency is the use of the Personal Allowance. This is a tax-free allowance on income, set at £12,570 for the 2021/22 tax year. Dividend income can be offset against your Personal Allowance, reducing your overall taxable income. However, it's essential to be mindful that your Personal Allowance is reduced by £1 for every £2 you earn over £100,000, until it disappears completely with an income of £125,140 or more.

While tax management may not be the most glamorous aspect of investing, it is nonetheless a vital component. A deep understanding of tax rules will empower you to optimise your dividend investing strategy and keep a larger portion of your investment returns. After all, it is not just about how much you earn but how much you keep that determines your financial success.

In the following chapters, we will delve further into creating a dividend investing plan, finding dividend stocks, understanding Dividend Aristocrats, and much more. But for now, let the essence of this chapter sink in: understanding the taxation of dividends in the UK is crucial for maximising your dividend investing success. Always remember, it's not just the gross return that matters, but the net return after taxes.

CHAPTER 6:

Creating a Dividend Investing Plan

When embarking on a journey, it is imperative to have a plan that details your destination and how you intend to get there. The journey of dividend investing is no different; it requires a clear and well-structured plan that guides your steps and actions. In the realm of dividend investing, your ultimate destination is financial security, and the vehicle that drives you there is the investment plan. This chapter aims to elucidate the importance of a dividend investing plan and guide you through the steps to create one, focusing on setting financial goals and assessing risk tolerance.

Setting Financial Goals

A goal is a dream with a deadline. It has been said that if you aim at nothing, you'll hit it every time. Without clearly defined financial goals, your investment journey is akin to setting sail with no predetermined destination. You'll drift aimlessly, tossed by the financial waves, without making any significant progress.

Your financial goals are your financial compass, the guiding north star in your investment journey. They give you direction, drive your investment decisions, and serve as a benchmark to measure your progress. Now, the question remains: How do you set these goals?

1. **Define Your Investment Objectives:** The first step in setting your financial goals is determining why you are investing in the first place. Are you investing for retirement, to buy a home, to fund your child's education, or to create a passive income stream? Your investment objectives will define the nature and timeline of your goals.

2. **Quantify Your Goals:** Once you've established your investment objectives, the next step is to quantify them. If your goal is to create a passive income stream, how much income do you aim to generate annually? If it's for retirement, how much money would you need to retire comfortably?

3. **Establish a Time Horizon:** Your time horizon is the estimated time you plan to start withdrawing money from your investments. It directly influences your investment strategy and risk tolerance. For instance, if your time horizon is long, you may be able to tolerate more risk and therefore potentially achieve higher returns.

4. **Create a Regular Savings Plan:** Now that you've defined, quantified, and timed your goals, the next step is to create a savings plan. How much money will you need to invest regularly to reach your goals within your established time horizon? You

might need to make adjustments to your current budget or explore additional income streams.

5. **Monitor and Adjust Your Goals:** Lastly, remember that goal setting is not a one-time event but a dynamic process. Regularly review your goals to ensure they still align with your financial circumstances and life goals. Be prepared to make adjustments as required.

Setting your financial goals is a significant step towards successful dividend investing. But like any investment, dividend investing involves risks, which leads us to the next section: risk assessment and risk tolerance.

Risk Assessment and Risk Tolerance

Investing is a balancing act between risk and reward. Every investment carries some degree of risk, and generally, the potential return of an investment is directly correlated with its risk level. However, the perception and tolerance of risk differ from one investor to another. Understanding and managing these risks is critical to creating a successful dividend investing plan.

1. **Understanding Investment Risk:** Investment risk is the probability that an investment's actual return will differ from its expected return, including the possibility of losing some or all of the original investment. There are various types of investment risks, such as market risk, business risk, interest rate risk, inflation risk, and liquidity risk, to name

a few. Each of these risks could impact the performance of your investments.

2. **Assessing Your Risk Tolerance:** Risk tolerance is the degree of variability in investment returns that an investor is willing to tolerate. It is a fundamental component in the investment process, often determined by factors such as financial capability, investment goals, age, income, responsibilities, investment knowledge, and personality. Understanding your risk tolerance helps you choose investments that match your comfort level with risk.

3. **Managing Investment Risk:** Once you've assessed your risk tolerance, the next step is to manage your investment risk. There are several strategies for risk management:

   - **Diversification:** This involves spreading your investments across various assets to reduce exposure to any single asset or risk. In the context of dividend investing, this could mean investing in dividend-paying stocks from different sectors or regions.

   - **Regular Review and Rebalancing:** This involves regularly reviewing your investment portfolio and rebalancing it to ensure it still aligns with your investment goals and risk tolerance.

- **Investing in Quality Dividend Stocks:** Investing in solid, high-quality companies with a track record of stable and growing dividends can also be a risk management strategy. These companies are often more resilient during market downturns.

4. **Risk and Reward Consideration:** The final point to note about risk assessment is the understanding that higher potential returns often come with higher risk. Striking a balance between risk and reward is an essential aspect of successful investing.

Creating a dividend investing plan is not a casual process. It demands thoughtfulness, careful assessment, and a deep understanding of your financial landscape. As the investor, you're the captain of your financial ship, and how well you chart your investment course plays a significant role in your journey towards financial security.

The setting of clear and achievable financial goals combined with an in-depth understanding of risk tolerance provides the blueprint for your investment journey. With these, the investor is well-equipped to navigate the financial markets, bolstered by a purpose-driven plan and a strategy tailored to their unique circumstances. After all, a well-conceived plan is a vital map that helps investors explore the exciting landscape of dividend investing, fully prepared to make informed decisions that align with their goals and risk tolerance.

CHAPTER 7:

Finding Dividend Stocks

In the investment world, having a well-thought-out plan is merely the beginning of your journey. The next step is to implement your plan, which entails deciding where you will invest. The process of finding dividend stocks is a crucial stage in your investment journey. This chapter will guide you through the crucial criteria to consider when choosing dividend stocks and provide you with resources to assist you in your research.

Before we delve into this topic, it's important to highlight a valuable piece of advice: the aim of dividend investing isn't simply to identify companies that pay dividends. The real task is to identify companies that have a high probability of sustaining and increasing their dividends over time. This requires more than just a cursory glance at a company's dividend history.

So, what exactly should you look for in a dividend-paying company? Below are a few key criteria that can provide a firm foundation for your research.

1. **Consistent Dividend Payments:** One of the first things you should examine is the company's history of paying dividends. Companies that have consistently paid dividends over a long period are more likely to continue doing so in the future. A

strong dividend track record indicates a commitment to returning profits to shareholders and a certain level of financial stability. To find this information, you can look at the company's dividend history on its corporate website or financial news websites.

2. **Dividend Yield:** Dividend yield is a financial ratio that shows how much a company pays out in dividends each year relative to its share price. It's an easy way to compare the relative attractiveness of different dividend-paying stocks. Remember, a higher yield isn't always better. An excessively high yield can sometimes be a sign of a company in distress. It's often more sustainable to look for companies with moderate yields, which are more likely to sustain and grow their dividends.

3. **Dividend Growth:** In addition to a consistent history of paying dividends, it's beneficial to look for companies that have consistently increased their dividends over time. Rising dividends can be a sign of a company's confidence in its future earnings growth. Moreover, it's an indication of inflation-beating income growth for you as an investor.

4. **Payout Ratio:** The dividend payout ratio is another important measure. This ratio tells you what portion of the company's earnings is being paid out in the form of dividends. Companies with a high payout ratio may not have enough earnings

to cover their dividends in the future, especially if they hit a rough patch. As a rule of thumb, a payout ratio that is consistently over 80% can be a warning sign.

5. **Earnings Stability:** A company's earnings can be a good indicator of its ability to pay dividends consistently. Companies with volatile earnings are more likely to cut their dividends during downturns. In contrast, companies with stable, predictable earnings are more likely to maintain and increase their dividends over time. Therefore, look for companies with steady, reliable earnings over a multi-year period.

6. **Financial Strength:** A company's overall financial strength is crucial in its ability to maintain and grow dividends. This strength can be assessed by looking at a few key financial ratios, such as the debt-to-equity ratio, the current ratio, and the quick ratio. These ratios measure the company's financial leverage and liquidity, respectively, both of which can impact its ability to pay dividends.

7. **Competitive Position:** Finally, a company's competitive position can impact its ability to generate the earnings needed to pay dividends. Companies that have a competitive edge—such as a dominant market position, unique products or services, or superior operational efficiency—are

more likely to generate stable earnings and therefore pay consistent dividends.

Armed with these criteria, you can begin your search for dividend-paying stocks. Remember, the goal isn't just to find companies that pay dividends, but to find companies that can sustain and grow their dividends over time. Therefore, it's necessary to look beyond just the headline dividend yield and examine the company's overall financial health and earnings prospects.

Now that we've discussed what to look for in a dividend-paying stock, let's turn our attention to where you can find this information. There are numerous resources available that can aid you in your research.

1. **Company Websites and Reports:** The first place to look is the company's own website. Most public companies have a section on their website dedicated to investors, where they publish annual reports, financial statements, and other useful information. Reading these materials can provide you with a wealth of information about the company's financial health, dividend policy, and future plans.

2. **Financial News Websites:** Websites such as the Financial Times, BBC Business, and Reuters can provide up-to-date news and analysis about companies and their dividends. They often have tools that allow you to screen for stocks based on

various criteria, including dividend yield, payout ratio, and dividend growth.

3. **Brokerage Reports:** Many brokerage firms provide research reports on a wide range of companies. These reports often include in-depth analysis of the company's financial health, earnings prospects, and dividend sustainability. They can be a valuable resource for investors willing to dig deeper.

4. **Investment Forums and Blogs:** There are also numerous online forums and blogs dedicated to dividend investing, where investors share their research and experiences. These can be a good place to get ideas and learn from the experiences of other dividend investors. Just remember, always do your own research and take online advice with a grain of salt.

5. **Financial Advisors:** Lastly, if you're unsure about doing your own research or if you just want a second opinion, you could consider speaking to a financial advisor. They can provide personalised advice based on your specific needs and circumstances.

In conclusion, finding dividend stocks requires careful research and analysis. By using the criteria outlined in this chapter and taking advantage of the available resources, you can enhance your ability to identify companies that can provide consistent, growing dividends. Remember, the goal isn't just to find companies that pay dividends, but to find companies that can sustain and grow their dividends over time.

In the next chapter, we will be delving into Dividend Aristocrats, which are a select group of companies that have a history of consistently increasing their dividends. But for now, remember, the quest for dividend investing is a marathon, not a sprint. Take your time, do your research, and always keep your financial goals in mind as you embark on your dividend investing journey.

CHAPTER 8:

Dividend Aristocrats in the UK

Investing, at its very heart, is a dance between certainty and uncertainty. Yet, there's an elite group of stocks that seem to turn the tide of uncertainty in favour of their shareholders. Their commitment to not just maintaining, but consistently increasing their dividends over the years, often come what may, has earned them a regal reputation. These royal entities in the dividend realm are known as 'Dividend Aristocrats'.

You may ask, what exactly is a Dividend Aristocrat? Well, let's delve into it. A Dividend Aristocrat is a company that has consistently increased its dividend payouts for at least 25 consecutive years. It's a title that isn't awarded lightly, as it denotes a company's strong financial health, robust business model, and, most importantly, its unwavering commitment to rewarding shareholders.

Aristocracy is not just about lineage; it's about character, resilience, and an unyielding commitment to uphold certain principles. This very sentiment encapsulates the essence of Dividend Aristocrats. The longevity and consistency of their dividend payouts are testament to their business acumen, financial discipline, and the endurance to weather various economic cycles.

Now, let's take a closer look at the Dividend Aristocrats in the context of the UK market.

Unlike the U.S., where the term was originally coined, the UK doesn't have a formal definition for Dividend Aristocrats. The U.S. Dividend Aristocrats are part of the S&P 500 index, and as such, these companies meet a certain market capitalisation requirement. In the UK, no such standard has been set, which means that companies from the FTSE 100, FTSE 250, and even smaller markets could potentially qualify as Dividend Aristocrats if they have increased dividends for at least 20 consecutive years.

Without further ado, let's introduce some of the stalwarts of the UK Dividend Aristocrat club. These examples will help elucidate the characteristics that have allowed them to consistently raise dividends, navigating the rough seas of economic upheaval with a certain poise and grace.

Unilever, the Anglo-Dutch consumer goods company, is a shining beacon within the Dividend Aristocrat cohort. Unilever has delivered a steady increase in dividends, reflecting its impressive record of stable earnings, global reach, and an expansive portfolio of brands that are popular with consumers worldwide. It demonstrates the ability to generate reliable cash flows, a prerequisite for any company to maintain and grow dividends consistently.

Next on our list is Diageo, a multinational alcoholic beverages company, renowned for brands such as Guinness, Smirnoff, and Johnnie Walker. Despite the regulatory challenges that the alcohol industry faces,

Diageo has managed to increase its dividend payouts for over two decades. Their strategy has been built around a powerful combination of popular brands, diversified across different alcohol categories and geographic locations, hence ensuring a balanced cash flow generation.

Relx, a global provider of information-based analytics and decision tools, showcases how a company operating in a unique industry can also achieve the Dividend Aristocrat status. The firm's portfolio of digital solutions across a diverse array of sectors, including legal, business, and academia, has allowed it to generate consistent revenues and dividends.

Similarly, Halma, an international group of technology companies, has been able to raise its dividend annually for more than 40 years, making it one of the top Dividend Aristocrats in the UK. The secret to its success lies in its innovative products that address various global issues, diversified portfolio of companies, and a strategy focused on sustained growth.

The key takeaway from these examples is that Dividend Aristocrats can emerge from any industry or sector. It's not the industry that defines them; it's their business strategy, operational efficiency, and commitment to shareholder returns.

But, it's also crucial to remember that past performance is no guarantee of future results. While these companies have an impressive history, they still need to be evaluated for future growth potential, current valuation, and their ability to sustain the dividend growth streak. In short, they must be put through the same rigorous analysis as any other stock on your radar.

By now, you may have gathered that the Aristocracy is an elite club, and it's not easy for companies to earn their place in it. Therefore, these Dividend Aristocrats should not be viewed just as stocks, but as businesses that exhibit resilience, stability, and a shareholder-friendly approach, earning them a worthy consideration for any dividend-focused portfolio.

Dividend Aristocrats represent a segment of the market that can provide a degree of certainty within the inherent uncertainty of investing. Their commitment to steadily increasing dividends paints a picture of consistency that can be attractive to investors who value reliability and income growth.

In the grand tapestry of investing, Dividend Aristocrats provide an element of stability. Their steadfast dedication to their shareholders is woven into the fabric of their business models, making them potentially valuable additions to your dividend portfolio. But, as with any investment, they should be chosen with care, discernment, and a careful eye on the broader market dynamics.

CHAPTER 9:

Dividend Reinvestment Plans (DRIPs)

Dividend Reinvestment Plans, commonly known as DRIPs, hold a special place in the heart of the dividend investor. These plans offer a convenient, efficient and cost-effective route to harness the magic of compounding. We are going to delve into the world of DRIPs, revealing their nuances, exploring their advantages and drawbacks, and deciphering how they fit into the broader tapestry of dividend investing.

The idea behind DRIPs is quite simple. When a company that an investor owns shares in declares a dividend, instead of the investor receiving a cash payment, the dividend is reinvested to purchase more shares in that same company. The process is automatic and continues to occur each time a dividend is paid, resulting in the investor gradually accumulating more and more shares in the company.

The quintessence of DRIPs lies in its automation. It allows the principle of compounding to be put into full effect, without the investor having to lift a finger. The investor's holding gradually increases with each dividend payment, which in turn leads to larger dividend payments, which then buy more shares, leading to an even larger dividend payment, and so forth. This process repeats itself over the long term, creating a virtuous cycle of growth.

To bring this concept to life, consider an example. Suppose you own 100 shares of a company priced at £50 per share. If this company pays a 5% dividend yield annually, you would receive £250 at the end of the year. Through a DRIP, this £250 would be used to purchase 5 additional shares in the company. In the next year, you would now have 105 shares yielding dividends, leading to a larger payout, and subsequently more reinvested shares. Over the years, this rolling snowball can lead to substantial portfolio growth.

This example serves to highlight the power of reinvesting dividends. Now let's explore the advantages of using DRIPs in more detail.

One significant advantage of DRIPs is that they encourage a long-term mindset. By automatically reinvesting dividends, investors are less likely to spend their dividends or be swayed by short-term market movements. This type of approach aligns perfectly with the philosophy of patient, long-term investing.

Moreover, DRIPs can be an excellent way to expand your holdings in a company without incurring additional transaction costs. Many DRIPs do not charge any fees for purchasing additional shares, which stands in stark contrast to the trading fees that are usually associated with buying shares in the open market. This cost-saving benefit can add up over time, especially for investors who are starting with a small initial investment.

Additionally, many DRIPs offer the ability to purchase additional shares at a discount to the current market price. While this isn't a feature of every DRIP, when it is offered, it can provide a compelling bonus to investors. Buying shares at a discount effectively enhances the yield of the investment, further accelerating the compounding process.

However, like any investment strategy, DRIPs are not without their downsides. It's important that we consider these disadvantages as well to form a rounded understanding of this investment mechanism.

One potential drawback of DRIPs is the lack of flexibility. While some investors may appreciate the automatic nature of these plans, others may prefer to have more control over when and how their dividends are reinvested. With DRIPs, you don't have the option of taking dividends as cash when you might need it, or using dividends from one company to buy shares in another.

Another consideration is tax. While the dividend payments are automatically reinvested, they are still subject to tax as if they were received as cash. This can lead to a situation where an investor owes tax on dividends that they never actually received as income. It's essential to factor this into your tax planning.

DRIPs also mean that you end up increasing your exposure to a single company over time. This can be a double-edged sword. If the company performs well, this increased exposure will lead to higher gains. However, if the company's performance falters, your losses could be more substantial. This could potentially lead to a lack of diversification in your portfolio, especially if you are using DRIPs for a small number of holdings.

Lastly, record-keeping can be a challenge with DRIPs. Since additional shares are bought at various times and at different prices, tracking the cost basis for tax purposes can be complicated, especially if the DRIP has been running for several years.

As with any investment strategy, it's crucial that investors weigh these advantages and disadvantages in light of their individual financial circumstances and investment goals. A DRIP might be an excellent tool for a young investor seeking to maximise long-term growth, while it may not be the right choice for a retiree who depends on dividend income to cover living expenses.

In conclusion, DRIPs offer a unique and powerful way to maximise the benefits of dividend investing. They exemplify the principle of compounding, enabling investors to grow their holdings without expending additional funds or effort. However, they also come with certain drawbacks, including lack of flexibility, potential tax implications, risk of overexposure, and complicated record-keeping. By understanding these facets, investors can make an informed decision about whether DRIPs are right for their investment strategy.

Regardless of whether you choose to use a DRIP or not, the overarching theme remains the same – dividend investing is a powerful strategy for long-term growth. And while mechanisms like DRIPs can enhance this growth, the key lies in consistently investing in high-quality, dividend-paying companies, holding these investments for the long term, and, wherever possible, reinvesting the dividends received back into the market. Through this process, even the smallest investment can grow into a significant sum over time, proving the old adage true – from little acorns do mighty oaks grow.

CHAPTER 10:

How to Analyse a Dividend Stock

Weaving through the labyrinth of the investment world requires more than just a whimsical approach; it necessitates a thorough understanding and analysis of the various factors that influence the potential of an investment. When it comes to dividend investing, this understanding is achieved through a detailed analysis of dividend stocks, to ascertain their inherent value and potential for dividend growth.

Our focus in this chapter is to break down this process into comprehensible steps, delineating the key financial statements to be reviewed and the crucial ratios that warrant consideration when analysing a dividend stock.

Let's start with the bedrock of any corporation's financial health - its financial statements. These are the primary source of data for analysing any stock, including dividend stocks. They provide a comprehensive overview of the company's financial position, performance, and cash flow. The three primary financial statements are the balance sheet, the income statement, and the statement of cash flows.

The balance sheet presents a snapshot of a company's financial standing at a specific point in time. It outlines the company's assets, liabilities, and shareholders' equity. It tells you what the company owns (assets), what it owes (liabilities), and the net value of the owners' investment (shareholders' equity). To a discerning investor, the balance sheet offers clues about the company's financial strength, stability, and liquidity.

The income statement, sometimes referred to as the profit and loss statement, provides a summary of a company's revenues, costs, and expenses over a period, typically a quarter or a year. It helps an investor understand how much money a company is generating (revenue), how much it's spending (expenses), and the resulting net income. This statement is essential for assessing a company's profitability.

The statement of cash flows, on the other hand, outlines the inflow and outflow of cash within a company over a specific period. It shows how a company is generating cash and how that cash is being utilised. It's divided into three sections: cash flow from operating activities, investing activities, and financing activities. Dividend investors, in particular, are interested in cash flow from operating activities, as it indicates the cash generated from the company's core business operations, which can be used to fund dividends.

Having covered the core financial statements, let's shift our focus to the key ratios that are crucial in the analysis of dividend stocks. These ratios provide a quantitative basis for comparing different companies and making informed investment decisions. The following are the key ratios to consider:

1. Dividend Yield: This is a fundamental ratio for any dividend investor. It's calculated as the annual dividend per share divided by the price per share, and it's expressed as a percentage. Dividend yield gives an idea of the return an investor can expect from the dividends paid by the company relative to its current share price.

2. Dividend Payout Ratio: This ratio is calculated by dividing the annual dividends paid per share by the earnings per share (EPS) for the same period. It indicates what portion of the company's earnings is being paid out as dividends. A lower payout ratio may suggest the company has room to increase its dividends in the future, while a high ratio could indicate the company is returning most of its earnings to shareholders and might not have much room to grow dividends in the future.

3. Earnings Per Share (EPS): This is calculated by dividing net income by the number of outstanding shares. EPS is an indicator of a company's profitability. Consistently increasing EPS may suggest that a company is financially healthy and possibly capable of increasing its dividends.

4. Price/Earnings (P/E) Ratio: This ratio is computed by dividing the current market price of a stock by its EPS. It gives an idea of what the market is willing to pay for the company's earnings. A lower P/E ratio might indicate that the stock is undervalued, but it could also suggest that the

market has concerns about the company's future prospects.

5. Debt/Equity Ratio: This ratio is calculated by dividing total liabilities by shareholders' equity. It indicates the proportion of a company's funding that comes from debt compared to equity. A high Debt/Equity ratio might suggest a company has a significant amount of debt, which could limit its ability to pay dividends in the future.

Each ratio provides a piece of the puzzle, but none should be used in isolation. A thorough analysis involves understanding the interplay of these ratios and other qualitative factors, such as the company's competitive position, the industry in which it operates, and the overall economic environment.

For example, a company may have a high dividend yield, which might seem attractive. However, if this is coupled with a high payout ratio and declining earnings, it could be a warning sign that the dividend is not sustainable. Conversely, a company with a lower yield but a stable payout ratio and increasing earnings may offer better long-term prospects for dividend growth.

In essence, analysing a dividend stock is akin to piecing together a jigsaw puzzle. Each piece, from the financial statements to the numerous ratios, forms part of the picture. Your job as an investor is to assemble these pieces, scrutinising the overall image while taking into account the unique intricacies and patterns of each individual piece.

It is a process that requires patience and diligence, but it is an endeavour that is undoubtedly worth the effort. For it is through this thorough and meticulous examination that you can discern a company's financial health, its capacity for sustaining and growing dividends, and ultimately, the inherent value and potential that lie within the dividend stock. After all, the essence of investing lies not in making quick decisions based on surface-level observations, but rather in making informed choices grounded on a deep and holistic understanding of the investment at hand.

CHAPTER 11:

Avoiding Dividend Traps

A sound investment strategy balances the pursuit of profitability with a robust risk management approach. Therefore, as we delve into the realm of dividend investing, it's crucial to understand not just the potential for fruitful returns but also the obstacles and pitfalls that might jeopardise your financial journey. A notorious pitfall in this area is what's commonly referred to as a 'dividend trap'.

Now, imagine a finely crafted Venus flytrap in the jungle. It is green, healthy, and quite appealing to unsuspecting insects. The insects are attracted to its nectar, a sweet-smelling substance that promises a sumptuous meal. However, the moment an insect lands on the flytrap, it snaps shut, trapping the insect within. Dividend traps function in a similar manner, drawing in unsuspecting investors with the promise of high dividends and subsequently ensnaring them in a precarious financial situation.

To be an effective dividend investor, we must not only identify the alluring nectar of high dividends but also recognise the potential danger lurking behind. We must develop the ability to discern between a true investment opportunity and a dividend trap. Let's explore how we might go about this.

Understanding Dividend Traps

Firstly, let's delve into what exactly constitutes a dividend trap. A dividend trap is a stock that lures investors with a high dividend yield. The high yield often results from a significant drop in the stock's price. While the high dividend yield might seem attractive, it can often indicate a company experiencing financial difficulties.

Why does this matter? Companies with declining health often cut or eliminate dividends when times get tough. When that happens, you, as an investor, are left with a stock that provides no dividend income and likely continues to decrease in price.

A quintessential example of this was the fall of Carillion, a British multinational facilities management and construction services company that went into liquidation in 2018. Despite posting high dividends prior to its collapse, Carillion was encumbered with £1.5bn worth of debt. The high dividend yield was a mere façade, masking the company's burgeoning financial woes.

Looking Beyond Dividend Yield

Recognising a dividend trap requires a willingness to look beyond the surface-level dividend yield and probe deeper into a company's financial health. Investors must consider the entirety of the picture, which necessitates a comprehensive understanding of the company's financials, performance, and the industry in which it operates.

An important tool in your due diligence toolkit is the financial statement analysis, which allows you to gauge a company's financial health. Looking at income statements, balance sheets, and cash flow statements can help determine whether a company has stable financial health or if it's teetering on the brink of insolvency.

The income statement provides valuable information about a company's revenues, expenses, and profits. A company whose expenses consistently exceed revenue is a warning sign. Similarly, a company with fluctuating or declining revenue could be in trouble.

The balance sheet gives a snapshot of a company's assets, liabilities, and shareholders' equity at a particular point in time. Companies with high debt levels relative to their equity may struggle to maintain dividend payments, especially in difficult economic times.

Cash flow statements can also offer valuable insights. A company can show a profit on the income statement while simultaneously experiencing a cash drain. If a company's operations don't generate enough cash to cover the dividends, it might be funding these payments through debt or asset sales, neither of which is sustainable in the long term.

Dividend Coverage Ratios

Another essential tool in your arsenal against dividend traps is the use of key financial ratios. Dividend coverage ratios can provide insights into whether a company can sustain its dividend payments. The dividend payout ratio, which we've discussed earlier, can give you a clear indication of the percentage of net income that is being paid out as dividends.

A high payout ratio may be a warning sign of a dividend trap. It might indicate that a company is returning a substantial portion of its profit to shareholders, which could potentially compromise its future growth. It might also signal that the company has limited financial flexibility and could struggle to maintain the dividend payout during financial or economic downturns.

Another useful ratio is the free cash flow to equity (FCFE), which measures the cash available to equity shareholders after all expenses, reinvestment, and debt repayment. By comparing the total dividends paid to the FCFE, you can see if the dividends are being covered by the cash generated by the business. If dividends exceed the FCFE, it could be an indication of a dividend trap.

The Dividend Track Record

Examining a company's history of dividend payments can also offer useful insights. Companies with a long and unbroken history of maintaining or increasing dividends are typically more reliable than those with erratic dividend policies. However, even a consistent dividend-paying company can become a dividend trap if its financial health deteriorates. Therefore, while the dividend track record can provide some assurance, it should not replace a thorough financial analysis.

Navigating Industry Trends

An understanding of the broader industry trends can help you spot potential dividend traps. Some industries are more susceptible to dividend traps than others. For example, companies in declining industries or sectors facing significant disruption may maintain high dividends to attract investors and maintain a semblance of stability. However, these high dividends might not be sustainable in the face of declining revenues and profitability.

Consider the plight of many traditional retailers in the face of burgeoning e-commerce. Despite the pressure on their business models, some of these retailers continued to offer high dividends, resulting in an inflated yield that masked the underlying challenges they were facing.

Investor Expectations and Sentiment

Lastly, keep an eye on investor expectations and sentiment. Companies with high dividend yields but poor stock performance could be experiencing negative investor sentiment. This could result in a self-perpetuating cycle, where poor sentiment leads to a falling stock price, which in turn boosts the dividend yield and makes the stock appear even more attractive.

In conclusion, avoiding dividend traps is an essential part of a successful dividend investment strategy. It requires a careful and thorough analysis of a company's financial health, dividend coverage ratios, dividend history, industry trends, and investor sentiment. By taking these steps, you can help ensure that your investment journey is not derailed by the seemingly attractive but potentially perilous lure of high dividend yields.

CHAPTER 12

Building a Diversified Dividend Portfolio

One of the fundamental principles of investing is diversification. "Do not put all your eggs in one basket," is a wise adage that applies particularly well to the world of investing, illustrating the importance of spreading investments across various entities to mitigate risk. This chapter will expound on this key principle, with particular focus on how to construct a diversified dividend portfolio.

Diversification – Why it Matters

In financial parlance, diversification means the allocation of investments among different economic sectors, geographical regions, and asset types. It is a risk management strategy that investors employ to smooth out unsystematic risk—the risk associated with individual stocks or sectors—in their portfolio.

The fundamental reason for diversification is encapsulated perfectly in a statement made by renowned investor Sir John Templeton, who said, "The only investors who shouldn't diversify are those who are right 100% of the time." As investors, we cannot predict with certainty which sectors or stocks will perform well and which will perform poorly at any given time. By spreading our investments across various sectors and geographies, we mitigate the risk of poor performance in one area significantly impacting our overall portfolio returns.

In the realm of dividend investing, diversification holds considerable weight. It allows investors to create a steady income stream from different companies that pay dividends at different times and rates, ensuring a consistent and steady cash inflow. It also helps reduce the negative impact of dividend cuts or omissions from any single company.

Strategies for Diversification

There is more than one way to diversify a dividend portfolio, and each method depends on the individual's financial goals, risk tolerance, and investment horizon. Here are a few strategies you may consider.

Sector Diversification: By spreading investments across different sectors, investors can mitigate the risk related to a downturn in any particular industry. For instance, a decline in the technology sector may not significantly impact a portfolio also invested in utilities, healthcare, and consumer goods.

Geographic Diversification: Companies are not only impacted by sector-specific events but also by geopolitical and economic factors. Spreading investments across different geographical locations can provide protection against such risks. For example, if UK markets are experiencing a downturn, a portion of your portfolio invested in US or Asian markets might still perform well.

Dividend Yield Diversification: Dividend yield is a financial ratio that shows how much a company pays out in dividends each year relative to its stock price. By investing in companies with different dividend yields, investors can balance income and growth. Companies with high dividend yields may provide better income, but they may also have lower growth prospects. On the other hand, companies with lower yields may have better potential for stock price appreciation.

Company Size Diversification: The size of companies, often categorised into small-cap, mid-cap, and large-cap, also matters. Large-cap companies are typically more stable and likely to pay consistent dividends, but they might offer lower growth potential compared to small or mid-cap companies.

Building a Diversified Dividend Portfolio – A Step-by-Step Approach

Now that we have understood the importance and strategies for diversification, let's delve into the steps to building a diversified dividend portfolio.

Step 1: Understand Your Investment Goals: Your financial goals are the cornerstone of your investment plan. They define your need for income, your tolerance for risk, and your investment horizon.

Step 2: Identify the Appropriate Allocation: Depending on your risk profile and investment goals, decide how to allocate your investments among different sectors, geographies, and company sizes. This allocation will form the base of your diversified dividend portfolio.

Step 3: Choose the Right Investments: Once the allocation is decided, the next step is to pick the right stocks, funds, or ETFs for your portfolio. Look for companies or funds that have a strong history of paying dividends, stable cash flows, and robust business models.

Step 4: Monitor and Rebalance: Once the portfolio is set up, it's important to keep track of the performance of your investments. Occasionally, market movements may shift your portfolio away from your original allocation, and it's important to rebalance it to maintain your desired level of diversification.

In conclusion, diversification is a crucial component of a successful dividend investment strategy. While it cannot guarantee against a loss, it is the most important component to helping you achieve a wide range of financial goals, while minimising your risk of potential losses. It provides a way to achieve a more reliable and consistent income stream from your investments, smoothing the bumps along the road of your investment journey.

Diversification does not eliminate the risk of experiencing investment losses. Stocks offer long-term growth potential, but may fluctify more and provide less current income than other investments. An investment in the stock market should be made with an understanding of the risks associated with common stocks, including market fluctuations. Remember, it's your hard-earned money at stake and taking informed steps will pave the way for a financially secure future.

CHAPTER 13

Investment Vehicles for Dividend Investing

As we travel on the journey of dividend investing, it's necessary to understand the various modes of transport at our disposal. Investment vehicles, that is the methods through which we make our investments, form the backbone of our strategy. They are the tangible means by which we put our hard-earned money to work. Whether it's stocks, exchange-traded funds (ETFs), or mutual funds, each of these investment vehicles has their unique attributes, advantages, and disadvantages. This chapter focuses on exploring these investment options, helping you to discern which would be the most suitable for your dividend investing strategy.

Let's start with stocks. Buying shares of a company makes you a part-owner of that business. When you purchase a stock, you have a direct stake in that firm. When it performs well, you do well. When it suffers, so does your investment. Directly investing in dividend-paying stocks is an excellent way to generate a steady stream of income. By owning shares in a company, you stand to earn from its profitability through dividends, a portion of earnings distributed to shareholders.

However, direct stock investing requires a keen understanding of the company and its financial health. While the allure of individual stock investing is strong, given the potential for significant gains, it does require a greater level of due diligence. With a direct investment, the burden of analysis falls squarely on your shoulders. You need to evaluate the company's financial health, market position, competitive landscape, and its dividend payment history and sustainability. It is not a light task, and not every investor has the time, the knowledge, or the inclination to immerse themselves in such deep analysis. Moreover, the risks associated with investing in a single company are high. If the company's fortunes fall, your investment takes a direct hit.

Our next vehicle, mutual funds, can be thought of as a collection of stocks, bonds, or other securities. A mutual fund pools together the money of multiple investors and allocates it across a diversified portfolio of securities, which are selected by a fund manager. When you invest in a mutual fund, you're essentially buying a piece of this diversified portfolio. In the context of dividend investing, income-focused or dividend mutual funds can be a robust choice as they specifically invest in a collection of dividend-paying stocks.

Unlike directly investing in stocks, mutual funds offer instant diversification, lowering your investment risk as your money is spread across several different assets. However, this diversification comes with a cost. Mutual funds charge a management fee, known as the expense ratio, to cover their operational costs. This fee, charged as a percentage of your investment, can eat into your returns over time.

Additionally, the performance of your mutual fund investment is largely in the hands of the fund manager. The success of the fund depends on their ability to select profitable investments, making it paramount to choose a fund with a proven track record of performance and a reputable fund management team.

Our final vehicle, ETFs, are a sort of hybrid between stocks and mutual funds. Like mutual funds, ETFs are a collection of various securities, providing the benefit of instant diversification. But like stocks, they are traded on an exchange and can be bought or sold throughout the trading day at market prices. ETFs often passively track an index, such as the FTSE 100, replicating its performance without the intervention of a fund manager.

There are ETFs specifically designed for dividend investing, known as dividend ETFs. These funds typically track an index of high-dividend-paying stocks. They offer the benefits of diversification and the convenience of trading like a stock. Additionally, ETFs often have lower expense ratios than mutual funds because they're passively managed. However, it's important to note that not all dividend ETFs are created equal. They can vary based on the index they track, their yield, their sector allocation, and more. As an investor, it's crucial to understand these differences and their implications.

But then, the question arises: how do we choose the right investment vehicle for dividend investing?

There are a few factors to consider in making this decision. Your level of investment knowledge and the amount of time you can dedicate to your investment strategy are paramount. If you possess a deep understanding of company analysis and enjoy doing your research, investing directly in dividend-paying stocks might suit you.

If, however, you value diversification and would like to avoid the intricacies of individual stock analysis, you might find ETFs or mutual funds more appealing. Mutual funds are especially attractive if you favour having your portfolio actively managed by professionals, albeit at a slightly higher cost.

Your choice also depends on your personal investment goals and risk tolerance. If your aim is to generate a high income and you are willing to take on a higher risk, direct stocks might be your preferred option. Conversely, if you're more risk-averse and want a stable income with the benefits of diversification, then dividend ETFs or mutual funds would be more fitting.

Investment vehicles are simply tools at your disposal. Each tool serves a different purpose and has its own strengths and weaknesses. When choosing your vehicle, it's essential to consider your individual circumstances, goals, and risk tolerance. Remember, there's no one-size-fits-all in investing. The best vehicle for you is the one that fits your unique investment journey, enabling you to travel towards your financial goals with confidence and clarity. As you journey on, may your dividends keep rolling in, and may your portfolio grow in strength and stability.

CHAPTER 14

Timing the Market vs Time in the Market

In this chapter, we delve into a fundamental debate that has long captivated investors and finance professionals alike - timing the market versus time in the market. We shall explore what these concepts mean and the inherent challenges, risks, and rewards of each strategy.

In the pursuit of maximising returns on our investments, particularly in the realm of dividend investing, it becomes critical to grapple with this dilemma. Shall we strive to select the most opportune moments to invest, or shall we commit to holding our investments for the long term, regardless of the market's fluctuations? As we shall soon uncover, the answer may not be as simple as you might think.

Timing the Market - An Attractive Yet Perilous Path

At its core, timing the market is a strategy that investors use in an attempt to buy low and sell high. Simply put, the goal is to purchase an investment when prices are at their lowest and sell it off when the prices peak. However, as alluring as this strategy may sound, it is a path fraught with risks and uncertainties.

To successfully time the market, an investor must make two accurate decisions: when to buy and when to sell. However, predicting the perfect moments to enter and exit the market is no small feat, as it requires not only a deep understanding of financial markets but also an ability to foresee economic and geopolitical events that could influence the market.

Market timing is a strategy that necessitates constant vigilance, exceptional financial acumen, and a dash of good fortune. It is akin to navigating a ship through a sea of uncertainty, where the winds of economic change can shift unexpectedly. Not only must the market timer continually adjust their sails to adapt to the changing winds, but they must also anticipate storms and seize upon favourable currents. Unfortunately, even the most seasoned navigators can find themselves caught in a tempest or stranded in doldrums.

This is not to say that timing the market is impossible or always ill-advised. Some investors have indeed been successful in their market-timing ventures. However, they are the exception rather than the rule. For most individuals, especially those new to investing, timing the market can be a precarious and stressful venture that often leads to more financial losses than gains.

Time in the Market - Steady as She Goes

On the other side of the debate, we have the concept of time in the market. This strategy is predicated on the notion of long-term investing and the power of compounding returns, which we discussed in Chapter 3.

As opposed to attempting to capitalise on short-term fluctuations in the market, long-term investors focus on the bigger picture. They aim to build wealth gradually over time, relying on the long-term trend of the market, which historically, has always been upward.

This buy-and-hold strategy significantly reduces the guesswork and stress associated with timing the market. Investors choose their investments based on sound financial analysis and future growth potential, and then hold onto them for extended periods, regardless of short-term market volatility.

It's essential to highlight that time in the market is not a passive strategy. It does not involve blindly holding onto investments, regardless of their performance. Instead, it necessitates regular monitoring and rebalancing of your portfolio, as well as a deep understanding of your investments.

However, the primary focus remains on maintaining a long-term perspective and not being swayed by the market's ups and downs. This approach fosters financial discipline and encourages investors to look beyond temporary setbacks and remain focused on their long-term financial goals.

The Case for Long-term Investing

When pitted against each other, time in the market presents a compelling argument over timing the market, especially for new and less experienced investors. This argument rests on several key pillars.

First, as previously discussed, accurately timing the market is exceedingly difficult, even for professional investors. Numerous studies have demonstrated that even those who succeed in timing the market once rarely repeat their success consistently.

Secondly, the risk of missing out on the market's best days is significant. According to an analysis by Fidelity Investments, if you had invested £10,000 in the FTSE All-Share Index over the past 15 years and stayed invested the whole time, your investment would now be worth £19,960. However, if you had missed the best 10 days in the market over that same period, your investment would be worth only £13,170. Missing the top 20 days would leave you with £9,320. This clearly illustrates the potential costs of being out of the market.

Lastly, the psychological aspect of investing cannot be overlooked. Market timing can be a stressful endeavor as it often leads to rash decision-making, driven by fear or greed. On the other hand, time in the market encourages patience and discipline, emotional attributes that are often associated with successful investing.

In the realm of dividend investing, patience indeed can be a virtue. Many successful dividend-paying companies have demonstrated stable, long-term growth in their dividends. Hence, investors who have held onto these stocks have not only benefited from increasing dividend income over time but also from the appreciation in the value of their investments.

As renowned investor Philip Fisher once put it, "The stock market is filled with individuals who know the price of everything, but the value of nothing." In the context of our discussion, it's critical to distinguish between the short-term price of a stock and its long-term value. While the former can be influenced by a myriad of factors and can fluctuate wildly, the latter is driven by the fundamental strength and growth potential of a company.

In conclusion, while timing the market may present attractive opportunities for quick gains, it is a high-risk strategy fraught with challenges and uncertainties. On the other hand, time in the market, or long-term investing, offers a less stressful, more manageable approach to building wealth over time.

As we venture further into the world of dividend investing, it's critical to remember that dividends are, by nature, a long-term game. The most successful dividend investors are those who understand the value of patience, the power of compounding, and the importance of time in the market.

CHAPTER 15:

Famous Dividend Investors and Their Strategies

A s we delve deeper into the intricacies of dividend investing, we stand on the shoulders of giants who have laid the foundation for our understanding of the financial markets. Throughout history, numerous investing maestros have shared their wisdom and experiences, lighting the way for those who seek to navigate the sometimes tumultuous seas of investing. The strategies of these financial wizards are numerous and diverse, each with its merits and demerits, its appropriate contexts, and applicability. This chapter presents a close examination of several of these remarkable investors, their strategies, and their relevance to the UK market.

One cannot broach the subject of investing without highlighting the substantial contribution of a man popularly known as the Oracle of Omaha. This particular gentleman is often seen as a guiding beacon in the realm of value investing, but his keen attention to dividends is less celebrated, yet of paramount significance.

Warren Buffet's investing philosophy centres around the tenet of buying companies at prices below their intrinsic value with the anticipation of long-term price appreciation. This is the essence of value investing.

However, a critical yet often under-emphasised facet of his strategy is his preference for companies with a consistent history of paying dividends. He appreciates that dividends, particularly those that are consistently growing, provide a consistent return and a cushion in market downturns.

One of Buffett's oft-quoted sayings encapsulates this philosophy succinctly, "Only buy something that you'd be perfectly happy to hold if the market shut down for ten years." This perspective underscores a longer-term viewpoint, one that aligns well with dividend investing.

For the UK investor, understanding Buffett's approach presents valuable lessons. Firstly, companies with steady, increasing dividends are often stable, profitable, and have strong cash flows - all hallmarks of a good investment. Secondly, long-term investing, a characteristic of most successful dividend investing strategies, mitigates short-term market volatility and allows the power of compounding to unfold.

One also cannot speak about dividend investing without mentioning the investment philosophy of Peter Lynch, the renowned investor and mutual fund manager. Lynch's approach, encapsulated by his phrase "invest in what you know," encourages investors to choose investments in industries they are familiar with or understand.

Lynch's strategy can be broken down into two aspects: the business and the stock. He pays a great deal of attention to a company's fundamentals, particularly its ability to sustain and grow dividends. For Lynch, a firm with a solid history of paying dividends signals strong business fundamentals and efficient management, attributes that are likely to result in solid long-term performance.

While Lynch is an American investor, his philosophy has significant implications for investors in the UK. Understanding the businesses you invest in can help in identifying those UK companies that have a track record of dividend payouts. Further, focusing on what you know can help manage risk, as you're more likely to grasp the potential pitfalls and opportunities in familiar industries.

Next on the list of dividend investing luminaries is Sir John Templeton. Known for his global investment approach, Templeton was among the pioneers of international investing. He held that the search for value should not be geographically limited but that investors should hunt wherever the potential for value exists. His investment strategy involved buying at the point of maximum pessimism and holding until a recovery. He believed that such investments often had lower downside risks and significant potential upside.

One often-overlooked part of Templeton's philosophy was his preference for companies that paid dividends. He believed that dividends provided a real return and protected against the ravages of inflation.

For the UK investor, Templeton's approach underscores the importance of considering companies beyond the UK that pay dividends. As we shall explore later in the book, this international approach can provide additional opportunities and diversification benefits.

It's also worth mentioning the approach of John D. Rockefeller, the American business magnate who famously said, "Do you know the only thing that gives me pleasure? It's to see my dividends coming in." Although known more for his business acumen than his investing prowess, his emphasis on dividends cannot be ignored.

Rockefeller's comment speaks to a fundamental truth of investing - the certainty of dividend income. Irrespective of market conditions, a company committed to paying dividends will provide this income stream. This consistency is appealing, particularly during market downturns when other forms of returns are hard to come by. This principle holds true whether you're investing in the US or the UK market.

The philosophies of these investing titans, while born out of the American market, hold universal truth for investors globally, including those in the UK. Their shared focus on dividends provides an added layer of stability and return in their portfolios. They understand that a company's commitment to returning profits to shareholders through dividends often signals a financially healthy company, one likely to withstand market downturns.

By employing these strategies, you will likely find investing less of a gamble and more a long-term, profitable endeavour. While these investors' strategies differ, the principles they adhere to - such as seeking value, understanding your investments, and appreciating the certainty of dividends - are foundational to successful investing.

However, remember that each investment should be evaluated on its merits and in light of your personal financial goals and risk tolerance. There is no one-size-fits-all strategy in investing. The investors we have highlighted in this chapter have their unique styles, and what works for them may not necessarily work for you.

Their lessons, however, serve as guiding principles as you navigate your investment journey. They are reminders that investing is not about seeking the next big thing or trying to time the market. It's about diligent analysis, patience, and, in the context of our discussion, understanding the undeniable value that dividends add to an investment portfolio.

The importance of dividends to these world-renowned investors underscores the central theme of this book. Dividends, often overlooked in favour of more glamorous investing facets, have a significant role in wealth generation. The UK market, with its rich history of dividends, provides an ample playground for those seeking to harness the power of dividends. So let's take these lessons forward as we continue to delve deeper into the practicalities of dividend investing in the subsequent chapters.

CHAPTER 16

Learning from Historic Dividend Crises

It is in times of crisis that we learn the most, and this sentiment rings especially true for dividend investors. The complex tapestry of economic turmoil, business uncertainty, and market volatility has unfolded several times in the last century, and each time, we come out more knowledgeable, more resilient.

While a dividend crisis may often come unexpected and unsettling, they are neither aberrations nor rarities. Economic upheavals are a part of the global financial fabric, and they have given investors valuable lessons to weather future financial storms. It's in understanding the past that we can prepare for the future.

To begin, let us delve into the tempestuous seas of the 1929 Wall Street Crash, an event that would forever shape the financial world. The euphoria of the roaring twenties came crashing down when the stock market went into free fall. The crash, the onset of the Great Depression, proved catastrophic for dividends. Companies strained under the financial burden, and shareholders saw their dividend income slashed. However, those investors who stayed the course during this turbulent period experienced the remarkable resilience of quality dividend-paying companies. The corporations that maintained strong fundamentals and prudent financial management rebounded strongly post the crisis.

Fast forward to the UK's secondary banking crisis in the mid-1970s, when smaller commercial banks experienced severe difficulties resulting from risky lending. This event led to a significant reduction in dividends across affected banks. In such an event, we learned that diversification can be the lifeboat that sees you through the storm. Not putting all your eggs in one basket and spreading your investments across different sectors can safeguard your portfolio from sector-specific downturns.

Coming closer in time, the early 1990s bore witness to the collapse of the UK's property market. The resultant recession had a profound effect on companies operating in the property and construction sectors. Many companies were forced to cut or cancel their dividends. Yet, amidst the wreckage, a few companies emerged stronger, reinstating their dividends once the market conditions improved. The key takeaway from this crisis is that a temporary halt in dividends does not necessarily spell doom. The ability of a company to bounce back and restore dividends is a testament to its underlying strength.

As we step into the new millennium, the dotcom crash of the early 2000s awaits us. A speculative bubble in technology stocks led to a sharp market correction, affecting companies across the board. But it was the tech firms that suffered the most, with many seeing their share prices and dividends plummet. The key lesson learned from this crisis was the importance of valuation. Paying heed to a company's intrinsic value rather than being swayed by market hype can save investors from potential pitfalls.

The financial crisis of 2008 is a critical chapter in the annals of financial history. A collapse of the subprime mortgage market in the United States set off a chain of events leading to a global economic recession. Banks and financial institutions, the traditional flag bearers of generous dividends, were hit hard, with many slashing their dividends. While painful, this crisis underlined the importance of a company's balance sheet strength and its capacity to withstand economic shocks. Companies with lower debt levels and robust cash flows were better able to maintain their dividends, even in the face of adversity.

More recently, the COVID-19 pandemic-induced recession brought about a slew of dividend cuts, deferrals, and cancellations. The crisis served as a grim reminder of the unpredictability of external factors and their impact on dividends. The companies that managed to sustain their dividends during this period were often those with resilient business models and the ability to adapt to changing circumstances. The importance of adaptability and resilience has never been more evident.

Navigating through these crises, it is clear that the path of dividends has not always been smooth. Crises have come and gone, each leaving behind invaluable lessons for investors. And the key threads that connect these lessons are prudence, diversification, intrinsic valuation, balance sheet strength, adaptability, and resilience.

It's vital to understand that the future will undoubtedly bring new crises, unexpected and challenging. However, by learning from the past, we can equip ourselves to handle future uncertainties. Rather than fearing a crisis, we should view it as a litmus test, an opportunity to separate the wheat from the chaff, the robust dividend-paying companies from the weak.

In the grand scheme of things, the ability to weather crises and maintain a steady dividend stream is what separates great companies from the good. These are the companies that not only survive crises but thrive in their aftermath, reinstating or even increasing dividends once the storm passes.

In conclusion, historic dividend crises serve as stark reminders of the risks associated with dividend investing. However, they also shine a light on the potential rewards for those who can identify and invest in the companies with the right qualities. Resilience, adaptability, and strong financial health are the hallmarks of such companies.

As investors, our job is to learn from these crises and to use the lessons learned to build a robust, crisis-resistant dividend portfolio. And in doing so, we aim to achieve a stream of dividends that can weather the financial storms and provide us with a steady income, come rain or shine.

CHAPTER 17

Dividend Investing vs Capital Appreciation

In the previous chapters, we've delved deep into the intricacies of dividend investing, dissecting its numerous aspects, from understanding the power of compounding to learning from historic dividend crises. Today, we'll explore another key area, one that often sparks heated debates among investors: Dividend Investing versus Capital Appreciation. In this discussion, we aim to bring more clarity to these two distinct approaches, aiding you in making a more informed investment decision that suits your financial goals and risk tolerance.

When we talk about investing, we often focus on two primary avenues of return: dividends and capital appreciation. Dividends are the profits distributed by a company to its shareholders, while capital appreciation is the increase in the price of the asset or investment over time. Both are powerful wealth-building strategies, but they follow different paths, and understanding their nuances is vital.

To start, let's dissect what each approach entails, their unique characteristics, and their potential advantages and disadvantages.

Dividend Investing: The Power of Consistent Returns

In a dividend investing strategy, you invest in companies that pay out dividends to their shareholders regularly. These companies are typically well-established, have a stable income, and are less risky compared to growth-oriented companies. As such, they're often favoured by those looking for regular income, be it retirees or those looking for a relatively stable, cash-generating portfolio.

Dividend investing has several advantages. Firstly, it provides a regular income stream, which is particularly appealing for those looking for cash flow, such as retirees. Secondly, dividends can serve as a cushion in market downturns, as even if the stock price declines, you still receive your dividends. Finally, dividends can also be reinvested, a strategy known as a Dividend Reinvestment Plan (DRIP), further augmenting your investment over time.

However, like every strategy, it's not without its drawbacks. Dividend-paying companies often offer slower growth potential because they pay a portion of their profits back to investors rather than reinvesting it into the business. Furthermore, dividends are not always guaranteed, and companies can choose to cut or eliminate them during financial distress.

Capital Appreciation: The Allure of Growth

Capital appreciation, on the other hand, is a strategy that focuses on the increase in price of the asset over time.

Here, you're investing in the potential of the company to grow, often foregoing current profits in the expectation of future gains. These companies often fall into the 'growth' category, including many tech startups, which reinvest profits back into the business for future growth instead of paying dividends.

The main advantage of capital appreciation is the potential for high returns. If the company performs well, the increase in the asset's price can exceed the returns available from dividends. Furthermore, growth companies often operate in high-growth industries, presenting the possibility of riding the wave of sectoral growth.

However, this approach carries higher risk. If the company or the sector fails to deliver the expected growth, you could end up with little to no return. Capital appreciation is also a less predictable income source, as it relies on selling the asset to realise the gain, making it less suitable for those requiring regular income.

Balancing Dividend Investing and Capital Appreciation

Understanding the differences between dividend investing and capital appreciation allows you to see that it's not about choosing one over the other, but rather about finding the right balance. Both strategies have a place in your investment portfolio; it's a matter of your financial goals, risk tolerance, and investment timeline.

A well-diversified portfolio often includes a mix of both dividend-paying stocks and growth stocks. This way, you benefit from the steady income provided by dividends and the potential high returns from capital appreciation. If you're more risk-averse or need regular income, you might lean more towards dividend stocks. If you're willing to take on more risk for potentially higher returns and don't require immediate income, you might lean towards growth stocks.

Pros and Cons of a Balanced Approach

Adopting a balanced approach to dividend investing and capital appreciation offers several benefits. Primarily, it provides a degree of protection against market volatility. When growth stocks are performing well, they can offer significant returns. Conversely, during market downturns, the income from dividends can help to offset any losses from a decrease in stock prices.

On the downside, a balanced portfolio requires careful management and regular rebalancing to maintain the desired level of risk and return. It also requires a broad understanding of both types of investment and the ability to research and select suitable stocks.

Final Thoughts

Both dividend investing and capital appreciation have roles to play in wealth creation, each offering distinct advantages and potential downsides. However, they aren't mutually exclusive strategies. Instead, they can complement each other within a well-diversified portfolio.

The key to effective investing isn't necessarily about choosing between dividend investing and capital appreciation but understanding your financial goals and risk tolerance. It's about constructing a portfolio that takes advantage of both strategies, providing the potential for both immediate income and long-term growth.

Remember, the best investment strategy is one that aligns with your financial goals, risk tolerance, and investment horizon. It's essential to conduct thorough research, continually educate yourself about investing, and potentially seek the advice of a financial advisor to construct a portfolio that best suits your needs.

So, as we've learnt today, dividend investing versus capital appreciation isn't a battle where one must emerge the victor. Instead, they're two sides of the same coin, each having its role in the realm of investing. By understanding their unique characteristics, you can harness their combined power to build a robust and effective portfolio, one that's geared towards achieving your unique financial goals. The world of investing is not black and white, and the true skill lies in navigating its many shades of grey.

CHAPTER 18:

Impact of Economic Cycles on Dividend Investing

As we delve deeper into our understanding of dividend investing, we realise the importance of comprehending the wider economic picture. The delicate dance of the economy, with its peaks and troughs, ebbs and flows, is something that we cannot simply dismiss as irrelevant noise. It has a tangible impact on our dividend investing strategies. To better appreciate these implications, we shall spend this chapter focusing on how economic cycles affect dividends, and subsequently, how we, as prudent investors, can strategise to handle different phases of the economic cycle.

Economic cycles, or business cycles, are the natural fluctuations observed in an economy over a period of time. They are marked by periods of expansion, peak, contraction, and trough. To put it simply, the economy does not always hum along at a constant pace. There are periods of acceleration and deceleration, of highs and lows, of booms and busts. Recognising these patterns and understanding their impact on dividend investing is an essential aspect of creating a robust and resilient investment strategy.

During periods of economic expansion, businesses tend to do well. Consumer confidence is high, unemployment is generally low, and people are willing to spend, which drives up company revenues. This increased profitability often translates into increased dividends for investors. It's a joyous period for a dividend investor as the companies in their portfolio may announce higher dividends, contributing to an increased income stream.

However, it's important to remember that periods of economic expansion, like all good things, eventually come to an end. When the economy peaks and starts to contract, things change drastically. Consumer confidence falls, spending slows down, and company revenues shrink. This contraction period can lead to lower dividends as companies try to conserve cash to weather the economic storm. In extreme cases, some companies may even suspend dividends altogether, a circumstance which can significantly affect the investor relying on dividends for their income.

But it's not all doom and gloom. The economy is a bit like a phoenix, rising from the ashes of the contraction phase, a new cycle of growth begins. As an investor, it's important to understand that while the economic environment affects a company's ability to pay dividends, it is by no means the only factor. Companies with strong fundamentals, good management, and a sustainable business model can often maintain or even grow their dividends, despite the challenging economic conditions.

Now, how do we navigate these economic cycles as dividend investors? The first step is understanding your own investment strategy and financial goals. Are you relying on dividends for income, or are you reinvesting them for growth? The answer to this question can greatly influence how you handle economic cycles.

If you are relying on dividends for income, especially if you are in retirement, it becomes even more crucial to invest in companies that can sustain their dividend payments through economic downturns. Look for companies with strong balance sheets, consistent profitability, and a history of stable or growing dividends. Such companies are often in defensive sectors, like utilities or consumer staples, which are less sensitive to economic cycles.

On the other hand, if you are reinvesting dividends for growth, you might have a little more flexibility. The fall in share prices during an economic downturn can provide opportunities to buy quality dividend stocks at a lower price. Keep in mind, though, that this strategy requires a longer investment horizon and a tolerance for potential short-term losses.

Another key aspect to consider is diversification, a concept that we have discussed earlier. Diversification across different sectors can help shield your portfolio from the impact of economic cycles. Different sectors of the economy react differently to economic cycles. While some sectors, like technology or discretionary consumer goods, may be hit hard in an economic downturn, others like utilities or healthcare may be more resilient. By owning dividend-paying stocks across a variety of sectors, you can reduce the risk of your dividend income drying up during an economic downturn.

In addition to diversification, maintaining a healthy cash reserve can also be beneficial. If you are relying on your portfolio for income, having a cash reserve can help cover living expenses without having to sell your investments in a down market. On the other hand, if you are reinvesting dividends for growth, a cash reserve can allow you to take advantage of lower stock prices during an economic downturn and buy more shares, which can potentially lead to higher dividend income in the future.

Let us remember the wisdom of the famed investor, Benjamin Graham, who once said, "The individual investor should act consistently as an investor and not as a speculator." This rings true especially when navigating through the economic cycles. Reacting impulsively to the cyclical highs and lows can often lead to poor investment decisions. Instead, focus on investing in quality companies with a proven track record of paying dividends and a sustainable business model. Make decisions based on sound analysis rather than market speculation or fear.

In conclusion, while economic cycles have a significant impact on dividends, they should not induce panic or lead to impulsive decision-making. Instead, understanding the economic cycles and their implications can equip us with the tools to make better investment decisions, help us build a resilient portfolio and potentially lead to a stable and growing dividend income over time.

Just as a skilled sailor uses the changing winds and currents to steer the ship towards its destination, a savvy dividend investor uses the economic cycles to guide their investment strategy. So, remember, while we cannot control the economy or the business cycle, we can control how we respond. And in that response lies our power to succeed as dividend investors.

CHAPTER 19

Inflation and Dividend Investing

Inflation is an economic reality, an undeniable force that shapes the contours of our investing journey. For those embarking on the path of dividend investing, it's crucial to understand how inflation impacts your returns and the measures you can implement to protect your portfolio. This chapter will delve into the realm of inflation, its effects on dividend income, and how to devise strategies to safeguard your investments.

When we speak of inflation, we refer to the rate at which the general level of prices for goods and services is rising, and subsequently, purchasing power is falling. In other words, as inflation rises, the pound in your pocket buys a smaller percentage of a good or service. For an investor, it's a silent thief, gradually eroding the real value of your returns if not correctly accounted for in your investment strategy.

The crux of the problem lies in the fact that dividends are not immune to the whims of inflation. While dividends might be rising in nominal terms, inflation may be quietly undermining the purchasing power of those payouts. This is why a well-rounded investor doesn't merely focus on the nominal figures but scrutinises the real returns—the returns after considering the erosion of purchasing power due to inflation.

Consider a company that increases its dividends by 2% year on year. At face value, this seems like a positive outcome; the investor is earning more from their investment. However, if inflation over the same period was 3%, the investor is actually making a loss in real terms because the purchasing power of the dividends they receive has decreased. This is an essential concept for the dividend investor to grasp.

Let's explore this idea further by looking back at the inflation trends in the UK. The UK has had periods of high inflation, such as in the 1970s, and periods of relatively low inflation, such as in the early 2000s. During times of high inflation, the purchasing power of dividends can rapidly diminish, leaving investors worse off in real terms. On the other hand, in periods of low inflation, the real value of dividends is more likely to be preserved.

The interaction between dividends and inflation brings us to the concept of 'inflation-adjusted' or 'real' dividends. Real dividends are the dividends that have been adjusted for inflation, providing a more accurate reflection of your returns. Therefore, when evaluating the performance of a dividend-paying company, one must consider not only the raw dividend figures but also how these dividends have kept up with inflation. Companies capable of consistently increasing dividends above the rate of inflation will yield real growth in your income stream and preserve your purchasing power.

However, we must address an essential question: how can an investor protect their dividend income from the ravages of inflation? There are a few strategies that can be employed, and they revolve around careful selection of your investments.

Firstly, investing in companies with a history of 'inflation-beating' dividend growth can be a sound strategy. These are firms that have consistently grown their dividends at a rate above inflation, thereby preserving and potentially increasing the real value of their payouts over time. It's noteworthy that such companies often have robust business models, allowing them to pass increased costs onto consumers and maintain their profitability even during inflationary periods.

Secondly, consider sectors that traditionally fare well during inflationary periods. For example, companies in the consumer staples sector often have the ability to pass on higher costs to consumers due to the inelastic demand for their products. On the other hand, sectors such as utilities may struggle, as they are often more regulated and might not have the flexibility to increase prices.

Thirdly, diversification can help mitigate the risks posed by inflation. By holding a variety of different companies, sectors, and even types of assets, investors can potentially cushion the impact of inflation. This strategy can ensure that even if some of your holdings are adversely affected by inflation, others might be positively impacted, thereby balancing out the effect on your overall portfolio.

Lastly, investment in inflation-protected securities can also be a tool for combating inflation. These are government-issued bonds where the principal is tied to an inflation index. Thus, when inflation rises, the principal of the bond increases, protecting the investor from inflation risk. However, such bonds often come with lower yields than their non-inflation-protected counterparts, and so they may not always be the best fit for a dividend-focused portfolio.

In summary, it's vital for a dividend investor to understand and prepare for the effects of inflation on their portfolio. Failing to do so can result in an erosion of the real value of your returns and impact your overall investment goals. However, by carefully selecting companies with a history of inflation-beating dividend growth, diversifying your holdings, and considering the potential use of inflation-protected securities, you can build a resilient portfolio that stands tall amidst the ebb and flow of inflationary trends.

Remember, as an investor, your primary concern is not the nominal value of your returns, but their value in real terms. And for that, you need to account for inflation. The pound today may not be the same as the pound tomorrow, and as investors, we must navigate our investment journey with this in mind. It's not an easy task, but with the right knowledge and tools, it's a hurdle that can be effectively overcome.

CHAPTER 20

Investing in International Dividends from the UK

When we open our eyes to the wider world, we don't just see a globe covered in diverse cultures, landscapes, and wildlife. We see an immense array of financial opportunities awaiting us. Among these, investing in international dividends is a prime area for consideration.

Why consider investing in international dividends? Because, as a UK investor, it's an opportunity to broaden your portfolio's horizons, diversify your sources of income, and potentially tap into higher yields that may not be available domestically. However, it also comes with a unique set of challenges and considerations, which require thorough understanding and careful navigation.

Investing in international dividends means purchasing shares in companies that are not based in the UK but offer dividends to their shareholders. These companies may be located in developed markets such as the United States or Europe, or in emerging markets such as Brazil, China, and India. The dividends they pay out, just like those of UK companies, are a portion of their profits returning to shareholders.

To illustrate, suppose there's a US-based company that pays out a dividend yield of 4% and an Indian company offering a yield of 7%. On paper, these may appear significantly more attractive than a UK company offering a yield of 3%. This, in its simplest form, is the allure of international dividend investing – the potential for higher yields and diversification.

However, an investor must remember that these yields are not guarantees. They are simply historical or declared figures. The company's ability to pay these dividends, both now and in the future, can be influenced by a multitude of factors that an investor needs to be aware of.

Firstly, let's take a look at currency risk. The dividends from international investments are usually paid out in the local currency of the company. As a UK investor, you'd have to convert these dividends back into pounds. Fluctuating exchange rates can have a significant impact on your dividend income. For instance, if the pound strengthens against the dollar, a US dividend will be worth fewer pounds. Conversely, if the pound weakens, that same US dividend will be worth more.

Consider this, if you invested in an American company that promised an annual dividend of $500. When you made your investment, let's say the exchange rate was $1.4 to £1, making your anticipated dividend income approximately £357. However, by the time the dividend is paid out, the exchange rate might have changed to $1.6 to £1. Your $500 dividend is now worth only £312.50.

Therefore, currency risk is a crucial factor to consider when investing in international dividends.

Secondly, understanding the geopolitical and economic conditions of the country where the company is based is paramount. These can significantly impact the company's ability to pay out dividends. For instance, changes in government policy, such as increases in corporation tax, could reduce company profits and subsequently dividends. Economic downturns, trade wars, and political instability can all impact the company's profitability and the security of your dividends.

Thirdly, there are tax implications to consider. Just as the UK taxes dividends, so do other countries. Double Taxation Treaties exist between the UK and many countries, which prevent investors from being taxed twice on the same income. However, the tax treatment can be complex and may require advice from a taxation expert or financial adviser.

Moreover, the administrative complexities can be higher for international investing. Not all shares in foreign companies are readily available to UK investors. Some may require a specific type of brokerage account or have limitations on foreign ownership.

Despite these potential challenges, the benefits of international dividend investing can be substantial if done prudently. One key benefit is diversification. By investing in companies located in different countries, you are spreading your risk. If the UK economy was to falter, having investments in other economies can provide some protection to your portfolio.

Another benefit is the potential for higher growth. Some emerging markets have fast-growing economies which can provide opportunities for significant capital appreciation alongside attractive dividend yields. However, these markets can also be more volatile, and the risk of loss can be higher.

In terms of strategy, a sensible approach for UK investors looking to venture into international dividend investing is to start with developed markets. Companies in countries like the US, Canada, Germany, and Australia can provide a balance between yield and stability.

Take, for instance, a global fast-food giant based in the US. This hypothetical company has consistently paid out dividends for over 25 years, growing its dividend every year. Despite being in the US, it is a multinational corporation with revenues sourced globally. Such a company could be a good starting point for UK investors looking to dip their toes into international dividend waters.

As you gain more confidence and understanding, you might then consider companies in emerging markets. These markets often offer higher yields and growth potential but come with increased risk. Always ensure any investments align with your risk tolerance and investment goals.

Lastly, it's important to consider how international dividend investing fits into your overall investment strategy. The principles of sound investing still apply - diversification, understanding what you're investing in, and a focus on long-term strategy.

In conclusion, international dividend investing offers UK investors a world of opportunity, from diversification to potentially higher yields. However, it is not without challenges - currency risk, geopolitical factors, tax implications, and administrative complexities all require careful consideration. But, with a thoughtful approach and an appreciation of these risks, the global dividend landscape can provide exciting prospects for boosting your investment income and achieving your financial goals. Always remember, though, investing is not about seeking out the highest yields blindly, it's about understanding the underlying risks and making informed decisions. Happy investing!

CHAPTER 21:

The Role of Dividends in Retirement Planning

Dabbling in the world of dividends doesn't limit you to just accumulating wealth over the years. It opens up an avenue that provides a path towards a comfortable retirement. You see, dividends aren't merely fragments of a company's profit that get distributed among its shareholders. They can be a source of ongoing income, especially for those in their golden years. In this chapter, we will delve deeper into understanding the role of dividends in retirement planning and how to structure your investment approach for a dividend-funded retirement.

To appreciate the role of dividends in retirement planning, we must first understand the concept of retirement itself. Retirement is a phase in life that everyone aspires to reach—a time where you get to reap the fruits of your hard work over the years. However, as life expectancy increases and pension schemes become less dependable, it's vital to consider alternative income streams during retirement. That's where dividend investing steps in.

The appeal of dividends lies in their ability to provide a steady flow of income. The crucial word here is 'steady.' With the end of regular salary cheques in sight, retirees look for something that could mimic the periodic inflow of cash, something akin to the salary they used to receive when they were a part of the workforce. Dividends can very much play that role, provided you've made sound investments in reliable dividend-paying companies.

Now, let's consider how to plan for a dividend-funded retirement. Dividend investing for retirement can be broken down into two phases: the accumulation phase and the distribution phase.

During the accumulation phase, your goal is to build a robust portfolio of dividend-paying shares. The primary aim is to reinvest the dividends back into purchasing more shares, thereby increasing your overall holdings. Reinvestment not only provides an opportunity to expand your portfolio but also serves as a practical demonstration of the power of compounding that we discussed earlier in the book. The more shares you hold, the higher your dividends will be, and this increased payout can be further reinvested to buy more shares—a snowball effect.

During the distribution phase, the strategy changes. Instead of reinvesting the dividends, you start withdrawing them to fund your retirement expenses. The dividends essentially become your income stream, helping you manage your lifestyle without chipping away at the principal investment. It's like having a golden goose that lays eggs—you enjoy the eggs without harming the goose.

A key aspect to remember is the timing of these two phases. Ideally, the accumulation phase should coincide with your working years when you have a regular income stream. You can use a part of your earnings to steadily build your dividend portfolio. The distribution phase, on the other hand, should ideally begin post-retirement when you need an income replacement.

The strength of this approach is the sustainability it offers. If planned and executed well, you can create a self-sustaining system that offers financial independence throughout retirement. You are essentially living off the 'income' generated by your investments rather than the investments themselves.

However, as with any investment strategy, it is essential to consider the potential risks and challenges associated with dividend investing for retirement.

The primary risk stems from the performance of dividend-paying companies. Dividends are not obligatory payments. They are distributed out of a company's profits, and if a company faces financial trouble, dividends can be reduced or even eliminated. Therefore, it's crucial to choose companies with a strong history of stable and growing dividends.

The impact of inflation is another factor that can't be ignored. With time, the cost of living increases, which means the purchasing power of a given amount of money decreases. Hence, you should aim for companies that not only offer a stable dividend payout but also have a history of increasing dividends at a rate that at least matches inflation.

Additionally, consider the tax implications. Though dividends can provide a steady income stream during retirement, they are, unfortunately, not tax-free. It's critical to understand the tax laws around dividends and factor in the tax liabilities when calculating potential retirement income.

Despite these challenges, the strategic allocation of investments in dividend-paying shares can lead to a rewarding retirement. The trick lies in creating a diversified portfolio to spread the risk and continually reviewing and adjusting your portfolio in response to changes in the market or your personal circumstances.

Let's bring all this into perspective with an example. Let's say, at the age of 25, Emma starts investing £500 a month in dividend stocks with an average yield of 4%. She reinvests all her dividends back into buying more shares. By the time she retires at 65, her portfolio would have swelled significantly, providing her with a comfortable sum every month in dividends alone, enough to support a modest lifestyle.

In conclusion, dividends can play a pivotal role in retirement planning. Their capacity to provide a steady and potentially growing income stream makes them an attractive option for those looking to secure their financial future post-retirement. However, like any investment strategy, it requires careful planning, diligent execution, and regular review. But with time and patience, you can indeed turn your retirement years into truly golden ones, backed by the reassuring stability of dividend income.

CHAPTER 22

Using Dividends for Passive Income

The purpose of investing is multifold. While some aim to accumulate wealth, others invest to safeguard their future, while yet others look to generate a steady stream of income. In this chapter, we delve into the compelling concept of using dividends as a form of passive income, and how a strategic approach to dividend investing can potentially result in a predictable and steady stream of income that requires minimal active involvement.

The allure of passive income is undeniable. It's a source of earnings that one receives regularly with minimal effort required to maintain it. This is income you can earn while you sleep, travel, or engage in other pursuits. Now, does the prospect of making your money work for you, without you lifting a finger, intrigue you? If it does, then dividend investing is a pathway to consider.

As a recap, dividends are payments made by corporations to their shareholders as a way of distributing a portion of their profits. These payments, typically made in cash, are a reward to shareholders for their investment and faith in the company. Dividend investing, the strategy of buying shares in companies that regularly pay dividends, offers the promise of a recurring income stream alongside any potential capital gains.

Investing for dividends with the goal of creating passive income is an age-old strategy that has worked well for many investors. And in an era where interest rates on savings are astonishingly low, the potential dividends offered by strong, established companies have a certain appeal. The process is straightforward. You invest in a selection of dividend-paying stocks, and then sit back and receive your dividends as they roll in. This allows you to earn money without having to sell your investments.

Let's now delve deeper into the dynamics of how this works. A company you invest in makes a profit. Out of this profit, the company's board of directors may choose to distribute a portion to its shareholders. These payments are your dividends. The frequency of these payments can vary, but in the UK market, they are usually made semi-annually.

The concept of passive income through dividends is built on this simple foundation. The income generated from these dividends can be used in any way you see fit. You can choose to spend it, or, as we've covered in previous chapters, reinvest it for further compounding. When aiming to generate passive income, however, the focus shifts to utilising these dividends as a regular income stream.

Before we delve into the considerations for such a strategy, it's important to understand the implications of relying on dividends for income. Unlike a regular salary, dividends are not guaranteed. They are subject to the company's financial performance and board decisions, both of which can be influenced by a multitude of external factors. It's crucial to remember this when charting out your dividend-based passive income strategy.

To generate a meaningful passive income from dividends, an investor would need a substantial initial investment. The more you invest, the more dividends you potentially earn. Let's take an example to illustrate this. Assume you invest £100,000 in a company that pays a 4% dividend yield annually. This would generate £4,000 in dividends in the first year. If the company maintains its dividend yield, you can expect this £4,000 every year, irrespective of the share price movements.

It's also worth noting that companies that have a consistent record of paying dividends are often mature and financially stable. They operate in established markets, have resilient business models, and are less likely to be disrupted by competitors or technology. This profile of company is often referred to as 'blue-chip'. Investing in blue-chip stocks can provide a level of predictability and consistency that is ideal for those seeking passive income.

However, a diversified portfolio remains a cardinal rule of investing, even when investing for passive income. Relying on one or two companies for your entire income can expose you to significant risk. What if one company faces a downturn and cuts its dividend? You could lose a significant portion of your income. It's therefore recommended to have a portfolio of dividend-paying stocks across different sectors to provide a safety net against such possibilities.

The amount of passive income you aim to generate also plays a vital role in shaping your investment strategy. A higher income goal might necessitate investing in companies with higher dividend yields. However, an unusually high yield could indicate underlying problems in a company, so thorough research is crucial.

Keeping an eye on dividend payout ratios can also be an effective way to gauge the sustainability of a company's dividends. A payout ratio that's too high may suggest that a company is returning too much to shareholders and not investing enough in its future growth, which could jeopardise future dividends.

It's also essential to consider taxation. In the UK, dividends are taxed above a certain allowance, so you'll need to account for this when calculating your expected income. Also, consider the use of tax-efficient wrappers like the Stocks & Shares ISA, where dividends are tax-free.

Lastly, monitoring your investments is crucial. While passive income implies 'set and forget', prudent investors keep an eye on their portfolio and the performance of their investments. Changes in company fundamentals, market trends, and dividend policies can all impact your income, and being aware of these changes allows you to adjust your strategy accordingly.

In conclusion, using dividends as a source of passive income is a feasible strategy for those who approach it with diligence and patience. By investing in a diversified set of stable, dividend-paying companies, you can create an income stream that requires minimal effort to maintain. Remember, though, that dividends are not guaranteed. They can fluctuate and even disappear. Hence, a degree of active involvement and ongoing learning is required to successfully navigate the dividend investing landscape and generate sustainable passive income.

CHAPTER 23

Real Estate Investment Trusts (REITs) and Dividends

Picture the grandeur of owning an assortment of properties – city-centre office buildings, bustling shopping centres, industrial parks, or residential blocks. Then, imagine the rent from these properties trickling into your account, almost like a steady stream of income, except without the landlord's responsibilities. This, in essence, is what a Real Estate Investment Trust, or REIT, offers to you as an investor.

REITs have been the answer to many investors' prayers, providing the opportunity to participate in the ownership of income-producing properties without the necessity of going out and buying commercial properties themselves. REITs offer you a way to invest in real estate that is as simple as buying shares in any other company.

Let's start with the definition. A REIT is a company that owns, operates or finances income-producing real estate. For a company to qualify as a REIT in the United Kingdom, it must meet certain regulatory guidelines. Perhaps most importantly for our purposes, a REIT is required to distribute at least 90% of its taxable income to shareholders annually in the form of dividends.

This chapter focuses on the REITs' relationship to dividends and how these can be incorporated into a dividend-focused portfolio. It is essential to understand that REITs can present a unique opportunity for the dividend investor, presenting potential benefits not readily available in other investment avenues.

Investing in a REIT, you become a part-owner in a portfolio of real estate. This may seem very similar to owning shares in any other business, and in many respects, it is. But there are fundamental differences that we must acknowledge and understand.

The first, and perhaps the most important difference, is the mandatory payout ratio. As previously mentioned, to qualify as a REIT in the UK, a company must distribute at least 90% of its taxable income to shareholders. This requirement leads to a generally higher yield when compared to regular corporations. This higher yield has significant implications for the dividend investor, especially those looking to generate a steady stream of income.

Consider this – a REIT that generates consistent rental income from its properties and subsequently distributes this as dividends to its shareholders can potentially provide a much higher yield compared to a corporation that might only distribute a small percentage of its profits as dividends. This characteristic makes REITs attractive to income-focused investors.

That said, it's not just about the yield. The stability of the income source is also an important factor. Rental income, which is the lifeblood of REITs, tends to be fairly stable. This is because rental contracts, especially for commercial properties, often span many years, providing the REIT with a steady and predictable income. Of course, this is subject to economic conditions, as well as the specifics of the properties and the tenants, but it remains a characteristic that stands in contrast to the more volatile income streams of many businesses.

But, like any investment, REITs are not without their risks. The mandatory distribution of at least 90% of income means that REITs retain less capital to grow their business, which can make them more reliant on debt or equity issuance for expansion. This reliance can lead to potential dilution of your investment if new shares are issued, or potential difficulties in times of rising interest rates if a REIT has to refinance its debt.

Also, while rental income can be steady, it is not immune to economic conditions. A downturn can reduce demand for property, pushing down rental rates and leading to vacancies. The value of properties can also fall, which could affect the REIT's balance sheet and share price.

Furthermore, although you, as a shareholder, will benefit from the REIT's profits through dividends, you will also share in the losses. This is true of any equity investment, but it is worth repeating here. If a REIT's tenants can't pay their rent or if the cost of maintaining the properties exceeds the income they generate, you, as a shareholder, will bear the burden of those losses.

And don't forget that the share price of a REIT can fluctuate like that of any other publicly-traded company. As a shareholder, you are exposed to the risk of price volatility, and there is the potential that you may not be able to sell your shares at the price you want, or in the worst-case scenario, you may suffer a loss if you need to sell when the share price is down.

An essential aspect to consider is the interest rate environment. Interest rates and the price of REITs often move inversely. When interest rates rise, the attractiveness of REITs, especially from a yield perspective, can diminish, and this can put downward pressure on the share price. On the other hand, when interest rates fall, REITs often perform well as investors seek out yield.

So, how does one incorporate REITs into a dividend-focused portfolio? Like all investments, REITs should be just one part of a well-diversified portfolio. They offer access to a specific asset class - real estate - that is otherwise hard to access for most investors, and they also provide a potentially high income return in the form of dividends. As part of a diversified portfolio, REITs can provide both income and a degree of hedging against other more volatile investments.

In deciding how much of your portfolio should be allocated to REITs, consider factors like your investment goals, risk tolerance, investment horizon and income needs. While REITs can be an attractive option for investors seeking income, they should not be viewed as a one-size-fits-all solution.

When choosing a REIT to invest in, some of the things to look at include the quality and location of the properties, the quality of the tenants, the occupancy rates, the track record of the management team, the financial health of the REIT, and the yield. Don't be fooled into thinking a higher yield is always better. A very high yield can sometimes be a sign of risk, and it is important to understand why the yield is high.

Remember, even though REITs can provide a steady stream of income through dividends, the principal value of your investment can fluctuate. As with any investment, it is essential to do your research and understand what you are investing in.

In conclusion, REITs offer a unique investment opportunity. By owning shares in a REIT, you get exposure to real estate, an asset class that has traditionally been difficult to access for many investors. The mandatory payout of a high percentage of income means that REITs can offer a high dividend yield, making them an attractive option for income-focused investors. However, like any investment, REITs come with risks, and it is essential to understand these before investing.

As with all parts of your portfolio, REITs should be chosen and managed in line with your investment goals, risk tolerance and investment horizon. They should form part of a diversified portfolio, offering both a potential income stream and a degree of stability, but they are not without risks, and these must be managed carefully.

So, while REITs can play a role in your dividend portfolio, they should be considered as one part of a broader, well-diversified strategy. With careful selection and management, REITs can be a valuable addition to your dividend investing journey.

CHAPTER 24

Investing in Dividend Growth Stocks

In your journey as a dividend investor, you'll encounter a wealth of opportunities, each with its distinct character and contribution to your portfolio's narrative. One particularly intriguing player on the scene is what we refer to as the "dividend growth stock." These are the stocks of companies that not only pay dividends but demonstrate a consistent increase in these dividends year over year. Let's delve deeper into this concept and understand the role these stocks can play in fortifying and growing your investment portfolio.

The appeal of dividend growth stocks lies not merely in the increasing dividends but also in the fundamental promise they typically represent. A company that consistently raises its dividend is generally one with strong financial health, confident in its future prospects, and committed to returning capital to shareholders. Such firms tend to have robust business models that enable them to generate significant free cash flows, a portion of which is regularly returned to investors in the form of dividends.

The Science of Dividend Growth Investing

At its core, dividend growth investing involves focusing on companies with a proven track record of increasing their dividends consistently. Dividend growth investors prioritize the growth rate of dividends, often over the absolute yield. For instance, a company with a modest yield but a high dividend growth rate may be more attractive to such investors than a company with a high yield but little to no growth in its dividend.

There are several reasons why dividend growth investing can be a successful strategy. First, growing dividends are a sign of a profitable and financially healthy business. Companies can only increase their dividends if they are generating sufficient profits, and the ability to do so over time indicates that the business is sustainable.

Second, rising dividends effectively provide an income stream that grows at a rate potentially higher than inflation, protecting the investor's purchasing power. This factor can be critical for those who rely on their investment income to fund their expenses, such as retirees.

Finally, a focus on dividend growth can lead to a concentration on quality businesses. Firms that consistently raise their dividends often have competitive advantages that allow them to generate substantial profits and cash flows.

Seeking Dividend Growers

But how do we identify these promising dividend growers? It's all well and good to say we want to invest in them, but spotting them in the vast universe of stocks can be challenging. Fortunately, the same financial discipline that allows a company to consistently increase its dividends also tends to leave other signs in the company's financial statements.

A good starting point would be to look at a company's dividend history. Companies that have consistently increased their dividends for a considerable period - say, ten or twenty years - are a good bet to continue doing so. This is not a hard and fast rule, and past performance is no guarantee of future results. However, a long track record of dividend growth does indicate a certain financial strength and a commitment to returning capital to shareholders.

Next, look at the company's payout ratio - the percentage of earnings paid out as dividends. A moderate payout ratio (generally between 30% and 60%) is a positive sign. It means the company is retaining enough of its earnings to reinvest in the business while also returning a significant portion to shareholders. A high payout ratio, especially one over 100%, could indicate that the company is returning more to shareholders than it is earning, which is unsustainable in the long term.

The company's earnings growth should also be evaluated. Consistently growing earnings are often the fuel for increasing dividends. After all, a company can only afford to raise its dividend if it is generating more profits. An examination of the company's earnings per share (EPS) growth over a number of years can provide insight into this.

Lastly, a firm's free cash flow (FCF) should be scrutinised. The FCF represents the cash a company generates after accounting for cash outflows to support operations and maintain its capital assets. A positive FCF means the company has cash left over after running its business and investing in its growth - cash that can be used to pay dividends.

Dividend Growth Stocks in the UK

Let's turn our gaze towards the home front and consider a few examples of UK dividend growth stocks. AstraZeneca, a pharmaceutical giant, is one such example. Despite the challenges of the industry, AstraZeneca has shown a commitment to increasing its dividend over time, with a track record to prove it.

Unilever, a consumer goods behemoth, is another shining example of dividend consistency and growth. Despite the fluctuations in the global economy, Unilever has shown exceptional resilience, underpinned by its wide array of popular brands. This resilience has translated into a reliable and growing dividend, much to the delight of its shareholders.

Utilities firms, such as National Grid, can also be sources of dividend growth. These companies operate in heavily regulated environments, where revenues are often more predictable. This predictability can provide the financial stability necessary to sustain a growing dividend.

Dividend Growth and Total Return

While the allure of a growing income stream is undoubtedly attractive, it's worth mentioning that dividend growth can also contribute significantly to total returns. Total return, as you'll recall, is the combination of capital appreciation and dividend income. Companies that can consistently grow their dividends often see their share prices rise over time as investors are drawn to the increasing income stream. This combination of rising dividends and capital appreciation can lead to impressive total returns.

Moreover, firms that regularly increase their dividends are generally less volatile than those that don't, leading to a smoother and potentially less stressful investment experience. This can make dividend growth investing a compelling choice for those with a lower risk tolerance.

Investing in dividend growth stocks can be a valuable strategy for both income-seeking and total return-focused investors. By concentrating on the dividend growers, you're focusing on quality companies with robust and sustainable business models - the kind of firms that can weather economic storms and come out stronger. As part of a balanced and diversified portfolio, dividend growth stocks can provide not only a growing income stream but also the potential for capital appreciation, contributing to a healthy total return.

By appreciating the power of dividend growth, we better equip ourselves to navigate the investment landscape, unlocking opportunities and building a portfolio that resonates with our financial goals. The pursuit of dividend growth is not merely a chase for higher income but a commitment to investing in quality firms that value their shareholders and show promise for a prosperous future. After all, as dividend investors, isn't that precisely what we're looking for?

CHAPTER 25:

Monitoring and Rebalancing Your Dividend Portfolio

" C hange is the only constant in life," is a phrase that rings particularly true in the realm of financial markets. The shifting sands of economies, industrial sectors, and individual companies necessitate a hands-on approach to managing a portfolio. This chapter is committed to guiding you through the process of monitoring and rebalancing your dividend portfolio to keep your investments aligned with your financial goals.

In a journey of a thousand miles, one must frequently take note of their bearings, ensure their compass is working correctly, and realign their course as needed. Similarly, once you have carefully constructed your dividend portfolio, monitoring becomes an essential task, albeit less often than you might imagine. It is through this regular assessment of your portfolio's performance and position that you can determine whether rebalancing is needed.

Portfolio Monitoring: The Necessity and Nuances

What is Portfolio Monitoring?

Portfolio monitoring involves periodically reviewing your investments to ensure that they are performing as expected. Monitoring is the equivalent of performing regular health check-ups. You wouldn't ignore your health until you are seriously ill; likewise, your portfolio requires regular attention to maintain its financial health.

Frequency of Portfolio Monitoring

There is a common misconception that portfolio monitoring requires near-constant surveillance of financial news and markets. The reality couldn't be more different. Continual vigilance can lead to overreactions to short-term market volatility. A healthy approach involves a systematic review of your investments, perhaps quarterly or biannually, depending on your comfort level and the composition of your portfolio.

The Monitoring Checklist

Effective portfolio monitoring should encompass the following elements:

- Performance Review: Compare the performance of your investments against your expectations and relevant benchmarks.
- Company Analysis: Review the company's fundamentals, business model, and growth prospects to ensure they remain sound.

119

- Dividend Check: Regularly confirm whether the company is maintaining, increasing, or decreasing its dividend payouts.
- Sector and Market Overview: Keep abreast of developments in the industry sector and overall market that could impact your holdings.
- Rebalancing Your Portfolio: A Timely Tactic

What is Rebalancing?

Portfolio rebalancing involves adjusting the weights of the assets in your portfolio to maintain your intended asset allocation. Let's say you started with a portfolio consisting of 60% equities and 40% bonds. If your equities performed exceptionally well over a year, they could now constitute 70% of your portfolio. Rebalancing would involve selling some equities and buying bonds to bring the portfolio back to its original 60/40 configuration.

Why Rebalance?

Rebalancing helps you adhere to your original investment strategy and maintain your desired level of risk. While it may be tempting to let your winners ride, remember that your original asset allocation was selected because it matched your risk tolerance and financial goals. Rebalancing ensures your portfolio doesn't stray too far from your original vision.

When to Rebalance?

Rebalancing should not be a frequent event. Too frequent rebalancing could lead to excessive trading costs and potential tax implications. A commonly adopted approach is to rebalance when an asset class deviates by a predetermined percentage from its target allocation. Alternatively, you could set a fixed schedule, for instance, annually or biannually.

How to Rebalance?

Rebalancing can be done in two ways:

1. Sell High, Buy Low: This is the traditional method where you sell the overrepresented assets and use the proceeds to buy more of the underrepresented assets.

2. New Contributions: An alternative method is to direct new investments towards the underrepresented assets until balance is restored. This can be a cost-effective and tax-efficient method.

Staying Steady in a Swerving Market

The goal of monitoring and rebalancing is not to eliminate risk, but rather to manage it. Remember, investing is a marathon, not a sprint. Over time, some investments will outperform while others may underperform. The goal is not to chase performance but to stick to your original strategy, adjusting as needed.

There is a pertinent quote by Benjamin Graham, considered the father of value investing, "Investment is most intelligent when it is most businesslike". Applying a systematic, businesslike approach to monitoring and rebalancing can help you stay focused on your financial goals, steer clear of emotional decisions, and enhance your chances of long-term investing success. With these principles in mind, you're now equipped to ensure your portfolio remains on course to meet your investing journey's desired destination.

Remember that the complexities of portfolio monitoring and rebalancing may initially seem daunting, but as with any other skill, it becomes more manageable with practice and understanding. By sticking to a disciplined approach, your investing journey will be less of a wild ride and more of a controlled, calculated venture. Maintain your course, assess your compass regularly, and let your investment journey be one of steady and sustainable progress.

CHAPTER 26

Dividend Policy and Corporate Governance

The bridge connecting the world of corporate finance and individual investors is the very subject of our discourse today - dividends. Dividends serve as the tangible thread, tying the interests of a company's management to its shareholders. These payments, quite literally, represent the fruit of a corporation's labour, a piece of its earnings returned to the investors who funded its endeavours. A company's approach to dividends, commonly known as its 'dividend policy', reveals a great deal about its financial health, long-term strategy, and fundamentally, its corporate governance. This chapter delves into the complexities of this policy, laying bare the integral relationship between it and the principles of corporate governance.

Understanding a Company's Dividend Policy

A company's dividend policy is its approach to distributing profits back to its shareholders. The distribution can either be in the form of cash payments or additional shares. This policy, often detailed in the company's annual reports, elucidates the proportion of net income that will be paid out as dividends and the part that will be retained for reinvestment. In essence, it outlines the company's philosophy towards its earnings distribution, shaping the financial expectation of its shareholders.

These policies can broadly be divided into three types: residual, stability, and hybrid.

1. **Residual Policy:** In this approach, dividends are considered residuals, essentially what is left after all profitable investment opportunities have been financed. Companies adhering to a residual policy typically have a volatile dividend payment pattern since the payouts directly depend on their earnings and investment opportunities.

2. **Stability Policy:** A company following a stability policy focuses on providing a steady and predictable dividend stream. The firm commits to a steady dividend per share, which it aims to maintain or gradually increase over time.

3. **Hybrid Policy:** This combines elements of both residual and stable policies. A minimum dividend is set under a stable policy, and additional dividends may be paid following a residual policy if the company's earnings permit.

Dividend policy shapes an investor's understanding of the company's financial strategy and future prospects. It also influences the investor's decision-making process and can be indicative of the company's overall stability and its commitment towards its shareholders.

The Relationship Between Dividend Policy and Corporate Governance

Corporate governance, defined as the system by which companies are directed and controlled, plays an influential role in shaping the dividend policy. This intricate connection has several dimensions that need unravelling.

1. **Board Composition and Dividend Policy:** The Board of Directors, responsible for making significant decisions including setting the dividend policy, significantly influences the dividends you receive as a shareholder. A board comprising mainly of independent directors is more likely to propose a shareholder-friendly dividend policy as these directors are less likely to have conflicts of interest.

2. **Management Philosophy and Dividend Policy:** The management's philosophy and attitudes toward risk also play a part in determining the dividend policy. Management more averse to risk may prefer a conservative payout ratio to keep retained earnings high, providing a safety net for unforeseen circumstances or future investment opportunities. In contrast, management with a higher risk tolerance may opt for a more generous payout ratio, rewarding shareholders with higher dividends.

3. **Shareholder Structure and Dividend Policy:** Companies with a concentrated shareholder

structure, where a small number of shareholders hold a large portion of the shares, may influence the dividend policy to suit their tax preferences or income requirements.

4. **Transparency, Accountability, and Dividend Policy:** Companies that adhere to high standards of transparency and accountability in their operations are more likely to have a clear and consistent dividend policy. They are often open about their decision-making process and make efforts to explain any changes in their dividend payouts, reinforcing trust and loyalty among shareholders.

5. **Regulatory Environment and Dividend Policy:** The regulatory environment can also impact a company's dividend policy. Companies operating in highly regulated sectors may have to adhere to restrictions on dividend payments, which will reflect in their dividend policy.

To encapsulate, a company's dividend policy not only provides insight into its financial strategies but also acts as a window into its corporate governance principles. A generous and consistent dividend policy might indicate sound corporate governance practices, implying that the company values its shareholders and is committed to rewarding them.

Dividend Policy: A Tool for Evaluating Corporate Governance

As an investor, one can utilise a company's dividend policy to assess its corporate governance standards. Several facets of the dividend policy can reveal information about the company's approach to governance.

1. **Consistency of Dividends:** A company that consistently pays dividends or has a track record of increasing dividends may suggest strong corporate governance. It indicates a commitment to returning profits to shareholders and a confidence in the company's ability to generate sustained profits.

2. **Transparency of Dividend Policy:** A clearly outlined and easily accessible dividend policy points to good corporate governance. It shows that the company is committed to transparency and has shareholders' interests in mind.

3. **Rationale for Changes:** Companies with good corporate governance will explain changes in their dividend policy. Whether it's a reduction due to investment in a significant project or an increase due to robust financial performance, investors appreciate knowing the reasons behind any alterations.

4. **Dividend Coverage Ratio:** This ratio measures a company's ability to pay dividends. A higher dividend coverage ratio may indicate strong financial health and effective governance, as it

shows the company's earnings are more than sufficient to cover its dividend payments.

It's important to note, however, that while the dividend policy can hint at the quality of corporate governance, it should not be the sole determiner. Other aspects, such as board composition, management's track record, financial reporting standards, and regulatory compliance, should also be evaluated.

The Role of Dividends in Corporate Governance: An Incentive Mechanism

Dividends serve an important function in corporate governance, acting as an incentive mechanism. This role of dividends stems from the 'agency problem' - a scenario where the management (agents) may not act in the best interests of the shareholders (principals).

Dividends help to alleviate the agency problem in several ways:

1. **Reducing Free Cash Flow:** Paying dividends reduces the free cash flow available to the management, limiting their ability to invest in projects that do not contribute to shareholder value.

2. **Providing a Signal:** Regular dividends provide a signal to the market about the company's health. Companies with robust corporate governance will pay consistent dividends, signalling confidence in their financial performance.

3. **Aligning Interests:** Dividends align the interests of the management and the shareholders. The promise of regular dividends creates an incentive for the management to perform well and generate profits.

In this manner, dividends play a critical role in corporate governance, acting as a tool to reduce agency costs and promote shareholder value.

Final Thoughts

The concept of dividends serves as a conduit, linking the realms of investors and corporations. It mirrors the efficacy of corporate governance practices and outlines the corporate philosophy towards financial management. Therefore, understanding a company's dividend policy and its relationship with corporate governance is integral for investors aiming to build a portfolio that thrives on the power of dividends.

In conclusion, dividends do more than provide a stream of income for investors; they also offer insights into a company's heart, revealing the principles and practices guiding its decisions. A company's attitude towards dividends, encapsulated in its dividend policy, can serve as a barometer of its corporate governance. Sound corporate governance, in turn, can foster an environment conducive to reliable and consistent dividends. Thus, the astute investor must pay heed to the intertwining of these two realms, using the knowledge to inform their investment decisions and create a well-rounded, fruitful portfolio.

CHAPTER 27

Ethical and Sustainable Dividend Investing

In the world of investments, the maximisation of shareholder returns has, for the longest time, been the principal goal. However, the landscape of investing has evolved, and now, we find ourselves on the cusp of a new age of investing - one that factors in more than just financial return. This paradigm shift encapsulates an approach that accounts for the environment, social responsibilities, and governance - often encapsulated in the acronym ESG. This chapter will explore the concept of ethical and sustainable investing and how it interacts with the world of dividend investing.

Understanding Ethical and Sustainable Investing

Before we delve into how ESG considerations can coexist with a dividend investing strategy, it's essential to first understand what ESG investing entails. ESG stands for Environmental, Social, and Governance - the three critical factors in measuring the sustainability and societal impact of an investment in a company.

- **Environmental Criteria** include a company's energy use, waste, pollution, natural resource conservation, and treatment of animals. It also evaluates the corporation's preparedness for dealing with environmental risks and their strategies to mitigate them.

- **Social Criteria** examine the company's relationships with its employees, suppliers, customers, and the communities where it operates. This includes the company's commitment to employee diversity, engagement in local communities, adherence to labour standards, and more.

- **Governance** pertains to a company's leadership, executive pay, internal controls, shareholder rights, and transparency in its operations. In essence, it examines how the company is run and how well it adheres to ethical standards.

Together, these ESG factors present a holistic evaluation of a company's business practices and their impact on the world. Investors interested in ethical and sustainable investing consider these factors in conjunction with the company's financial metrics to make investment decisions.

The Intersection of ESG Investing and Dividends

Now that we have a clearer understanding of what ESG investing involves, the question is, how does this relate to our pursuit of dividends? In fact, these two seemingly disparate aspects of investing are more intertwined than you might think. Several reasons explain this intersection:

1. **Long-Term Focus:** Dividend investing, at its core, is a long-term strategy. Ethical and sustainable practices align well with this long-term focus as companies that prioritise ESG factors are typically looking beyond short-term profits to a more sustainable future. This long-term approach can also translate into steady, reliable dividends over time.

2. **Lower Risk:** Companies that score well on ESG criteria are often seen as lower risk. They're more likely to be compliant with regulations, less likely to be hit with fines or lawsuits, and more likely to be resilient in the face of market volatility. Lower risk can contribute to stable earnings, which, in turn, support reliable dividend payments.

3. **Resilience in Market Downturns:** During periods of market stress, ESG-focused companies tend to be more resilient, and thus, more likely to maintain their dividend payments.

4. **Reputation and Brand Value:** Companies with robust ESG practices often enjoy a good reputation and strong brand value, factors that can translate into increased customer loyalty, better pricing power, and ultimately, higher profits and dividends.

Therefore, integrating ESG factors into your dividend investing strategy can lead to an alignment of both financial returns and sustainability goals.

Finding Ethical and Sustainable Dividend Stocks

The next logical question is, how does one find ethical and sustainable dividend stocks? Here are some pointers to help you find these companies:

1. **Look at ESG Ratings:** Several agencies provide ESG ratings for companies. These ratings, often available to the public, are a good starting point for assessing a company's commitment to ethical and sustainable practices.

2. **Examine Company Reports and Statements:** Many companies now produce sustainability reports in addition to their annual financial reports. These can provide valuable insights into a company's ESG efforts. It's also worthwhile to examine their mission and value statements for commitments to sustainability.

3. **Use Dedicated ESG Research Platforms:** Several platforms focus specifically on ESG research and provide a wealth of data on companies' ESG performance. Some of these platforms may require a subscription, but the in-depth analysis they provide can be invaluable.

4. **Consider Companies in Sustainable Industries:** Companies in certain sectors, such as renewable energy, are more likely to align with ESG criteria. However, be sure to carry out thorough research as not every company within these sectors will necessarily be ESG compliant.

While you research potential investments, remember to keep dividend factors in mind. Look at the company's dividend yield, payout ratio, and history of dividend payments. Remember, a sustainable dividend-paying company is one that balances both its ESG commitments and its obligations to shareholders.

Constructing an Ethical and Sustainable Dividend Portfolio

Now that you've identified potential ethical and sustainable dividend stocks, it's time to construct your portfolio. Here are some key points to consider:

1. **Diversification:** As with any investment strategy, diversification is crucial. This principle applies both to the sectors you invest in and the ESG issues you focus on. A balanced portfolio will spread across different industries and address a variety of ESG factors.

2. **Consistent Reassessment:** ESG ratings can change over time as companies alter their practices. Similarly, a company's dividend health can vary. Regularly reassess your portfolio to ensure that your investments continue to align with your ethical, sustainable, and financial goals.

3. **Patience and Persistence:** Remember, both dividend investing and ESG investing are long-term strategies. Stay patient and persistent, and the rewards can be significant.

Navigating the Challenges

While ethical and sustainable dividend investing offers numerous benefits, it's not without its challenges. One of the most significant is the lack of standardised ESG reporting. Different rating agencies may use varying criteria, leading to discrepancies in ESG scores. It's also worth noting that ESG reports provided by companies themselves may present a positive bias.

Another challenge lies in defining what is 'ethical' and 'sustainable'. These concepts can be subjective and may vary from investor to investor. It's important to clarify your own values and priorities before embarking on this investment path.

Despite these challenges, the trend towards ESG investing continues to grow, and with it, the data and tools available to investors improve. It's becoming easier to align your investment strategy with your ethical and sustainability values.

In conclusion, it's clear that ethical and sustainable considerations can comfortably coexist with a dividend investing strategy. By integrating ESG factors into your investment decisions, you can work towards a future that is both financially rewarding and sustainable. With careful research and mindful investing, you can contribute towards a better world while reaping the benefits of steady dividend income.

CHAPTER 28

Dividends vs Buybacks

The world of finance and investing is complex and multifaceted, providing numerous ways for corporations to return value to their shareholders. Dividends and share buybacks represent two of the most prominent mechanisms used by companies in this pursuit. This chapter aims to shed light on these two methods, explaining their purpose, their impact on investors, and how to navigate the sometimes complex interplay between the two in the context of your dividend investing strategy.

The Role of Dividends and Share Buybacks

Let's begin by defining what dividends and share buybacks are and their respective roles in a company's financial strategy.

Dividends, as you already know from the preceding chapters, represent a portion of a company's earnings that it distributes to its shareholders. Companies use dividends as a way of directly rewarding their investors, with the amount paid often reflecting the business's profitability and financial health.

On the other hand, a **share buyback** (or share repurchase) is a corporate action in which a company buys back its own shares from the marketplace. The process reduces the number of outstanding shares, which can increase the value of the remaining shares, increase earnings per share (EPS), and show confidence in the company's prospects.

Dividends vs Buybacks: An Overview

To understand how dividends and buybacks affect shareholders, let's examine the key characteristics of each:

Dividends:

1. **Immediate Return:** Dividends provide an immediate return to shareholders, delivered in the form of cash payments.

2. **Income Focus:** Dividends are often favoured by income-focused investors, including retirees who may rely on dividends for a regular income stream.

3. **Tax Implications:** In the UK, dividends are subject to taxation. However, as detailed in chapter 5, certain tax-efficient accounts and strategies can be used to minimise the tax impact.

Share Buybacks:

1. **Potential Share Price Increase:** As buybacks reduce the number of outstanding shares, they can potentially increase the share price and, therefore, the value of shareholders' investments.

2. **EPS Enhancement:** By reducing the number of shares in circulation, buybacks can increase the earnings per share (EPS) even without an increase in total earnings. This may improve the company's attractiveness to investors.

3. **Tax Efficiency:** Share buybacks can be more tax-efficient than dividends. When a company buys back its shares, the capital gains aren't realised until investors sell their shares, potentially deferring tax obligations.

Interplay Between Dividends and Buybacks

It's important to note that dividends and buybacks are not mutually exclusive and can coexist as part of a company's broader capital return strategy. Some companies might use a combination of both, adjusting the mix based on their cash flow, business prospects, and the market environment.

This interplay between dividends and buybacks can sometimes make interpreting a company's financial health and investment attractiveness more complex. For instance, if a company is increasing its dividends while also engaging in extensive buybacks, this could be a positive sign of strong cash flow and a management team confident in the business's future.

On the other hand, a company might increase buybacks while cutting dividends, which could signal different things. It could be a strategic move to improve tax efficiency and shareholder value, or it might be due to cash flow issues, which make it hard to commit to ongoing dividend payments.

Understanding the motives behind these actions requires thorough analysis and an understanding of the broader context, including the company's performance, the industry dynamics, and the market conditions.

Evaluating Dividends and Buybacks

When considering dividends and buybacks as part of your investment strategy, it's crucial to delve beneath the surface and understand the implications and motivations behind these decisions. Here are a few key factors to consider:

Company's Financial Health: First and foremost, scrutinise the company's financial statements. Is the company generating sufficient cash flow to support its dividend payments and buybacks? If a company is borrowing heavily to fund these, it could be a warning sign.

Dividend Coverage: Always check the company's dividend coverage ratio (earnings per share divided by dividends per share). This ratio indicates the company's ability to cover its dividend payments. A higher ratio is generally better.

Buyback Efficiency: When it comes to buybacks, consider the company's buyback yield (the percentage of the company's market cap that has been bought back over the last year) and its efficiency. Has the company been buying back shares when the stock is undervalued? If it's buying back overvalued shares, it might be destroying shareholder value rather than adding to it.

Management's Track Record and Transparency: Look at the management team's track record in making capital allocation decisions. Are they transparent about their reasons for choosing dividends, buybacks, or a mix of both? Clear and logical reasoning can inspire confidence.

Dividends or Buybacks: Which is Better?

The answer to this question depends on individual circumstances and investment goals. If you're an investor seeking regular income, perhaps to fund your retirement, then dividends might be more attractive. If you're in a higher tax bracket, the capital gains from share buybacks might be more appealing due to their potential tax efficiency.

It's also worth considering the signalling effect of dividends and buybacks. A consistent history of regular, growing dividends signals a company's financial health and confidence in its future earnings, which might be attractive to long-term, income-focused investors.

On the other hand, a share buyback might signal that the company's management believes the stock is undervalued – which could be an attractive proposition for investors seeking capital appreciation.

In reality, many successful companies use a combination of both dividends and buybacks to return capital to their shareholders. This blended approach can allow companies to maintain an attractive dividend yield for income-focused investors while also using buybacks to optimise capital structure, improve EPS and potentially enhance overall shareholder value.

Conclusion

Dividends and buybacks represent two different but often complementary ways in which companies can return capital to shareholders. As a dividend investor, it's essential to understand these mechanisms, how they interact, and what they signal about a company's financial health and future prospects.

Always remember that whether a company chooses to pay dividends, buy back shares, or a mix of both should not be the sole factor in your investment decision. It's just one part of the bigger picture. As with all aspects of investing, thorough research, careful analysis and a focus on your individual financial goals and risk tolerance should guide your decisions.

Understanding the interplay between dividends and buybacks can enhance your ability to make informed investment decisions and, ultimately, help you build a successful, income-generating portfolio. As you navigate the world of dividend investing, keep in mind the dual tools companies have at their disposal to return capital to you, the shareholder. Use this knowledge to your advantage to better interpret corporate actions and their implications for your investments.

CHAPTER 29

Advanced Dividend Concepts

As we delve deeper into the world of dividend investing, we encounter concepts that may initially seem more complex. They are the bedrock on which intelligent investment decisions are made. In this chapter, we'll discuss ex-dividend dates, dividend cover, and scrip dividends. Understanding these will enhance your knowledge and add sophistication to your investment strategy.

Let us begin with the concept of an 'ex-dividend' date. It's a date that one should circle in their investment calendar.

An ex-dividend date is simply the date upon which a company's shares cease to bear the right to the most recently declared dividend. Once a dividend has been declared, a company will set an ex-dividend date. If you purchase shares before the ex-dividend date, you'll receive the upcoming dividend. Conversely, if you purchase shares on or after the ex-dividend date, you won't receive the upcoming dividend.

As a simple illustration, let's imagine a company called Alpha Corp. It declares a dividend on 1st July. The ex-dividend date is set for 15th July. If you purchase shares of Alpha Corp on 14th July, you will receive the declared dividend. But if you purchase on 15th July, the day of the ex-dividend date, you are not eligible for the recently declared dividend.

While it might seem like a good strategy to purchase shares just before the ex-dividend date and then sell them just after, in practice, this is often unprofitable. The market adjusts for the dividend payment, and the share price typically drops by roughly the amount of the dividend on the ex-dividend date. Therefore, an investor cannot reap a windfall profit by merely buying and selling around the ex-dividend date.

Next, we have 'dividend cover,' a financial metric that adds nuance to the discussion of dividend sustainability. It's a ratio that indicates the number of times a company can pay dividends to shareholders out of its net profits. It's calculated by dividing a company's net profit by the total dividend paid out.

For instance, if Beta Corp. has a net profit of £1 million and pays out £200,000 in dividends, its dividend cover is £1,000,000 divided by £200,000, which equals 5. This suggests that Beta Corp.'s dividends are well covered and sustainable given its current earnings level.

If a company's dividend cover is less than 1, it indicates that the company is paying out more in dividends than it's earning, which may not be sustainable in the long run. For dividend investors, a higher dividend cover ratio is generally preferable, as it signifies a higher degree of dividend safety.

But beware, a high dividend cover may also suggest that a company is not returning as much profit to shareholders as it could. As with most things in investing, balance is key.

Lastly, we turn our attention to 'scrip dividends.' A scrip dividend is a dividend payment made in the form of additional shares in the company, rather than as a cash payout.

Consider Gamma Ltd. It decides to issue a scrip dividend. Instead of receiving a cash dividend, shareholders receive additional shares in Gamma Ltd. proportionate to their current shareholding.

There are a number of reasons why a company may choose to issue a scrip dividend. It may wish to retain its cash for further investment, or it may not have sufficient cash to hand. From the investor's point of view, scrip dividends can be advantageous as they increase the investor's shareholding without any additional investment. However, they do not provide the immediate cash benefit that a standard cash dividend does. It's an option that merits consideration based on an investor's individual financial circumstances and the company's performance.

It's also important to note that scrip dividends are not free shares. They have a value, which forms part of the total dividends received in the tax year, and may therefore affect your tax liability.

Understanding these advanced concepts – the ex-dividend date, dividend cover, and scrip dividends – can help you make informed decisions about your investments. It deepens your understanding of the mechanics of dividends and provides further insights into company finances and shareholder policies. As we've seen throughout this guide, knowledge is an investor's most powerful tool.

By incorporating these advanced concepts into your investment strategy, you are not merely adding arrows to your quiver. You're refining your aim, making it possible to hit your investment targets with more precision. After all, dividend investing, at its heart, is about building wealth methodically and strategically over the long term. These concepts are an integral part of that journey.

While these concepts may seem complex at first, understanding them is a solid step toward mastering dividend investing. They illustrate how a company chooses to reward its shareholders, providing key insights into a company's financial health. Keep these concepts in mind, and they'll provide valuable guidance as you continue to build and refine your dividend portfolio.

CHAPTER 30

Conclusion - The Future of Dividend Investing in the UK

Dividend investing, much like life itself, remains in a constant state of flux. As a prism reflects the varied colours of the rainbow, so too does dividend investing reveal its multitude of nuances under the ever-changing light of the global financial landscape.

In this final chapter, we shall immerse ourselves in the speculative realm of the future, focusing on what the coming years might hold for the fascinating field of dividend investing in the United Kingdom.

In this endeavour, however, we must keep one thing at the forefront of our minds: the act of prediction is as much an art as it is a science. It is akin to sailing in uncharted waters; a course needs to be plotted with the aid of available instruments, but the unpredictable winds and tides of economic forces can alter the path significantly. Therefore, our objective here isn't to provide an exact map, but rather to prepare you to navigate any potential storms and ride the wind currents to your advantage.

Let's begin by examining some of the broader economic trends that might shape the future of dividend investing in the UK. The most prominent amongst these are the continuing digitisation of the economy, shifting demographics, environmental concerns, and the uncertainties posed by globalisation and political factors.

The Digital Revolution and Dividend Investing

The profound transformation that digitisation has wrought on economies worldwide is indisputable. Businesses across industries have had to evolve to stay afloat in these digital waters, and those who have succeeded are now reaping the benefits.

In the context of dividend investing, this digital revolution has a two-fold impact. On one hand, it has led to the rise of new sectors and industries that are highly profitable and capable of paying attractive dividends. Information technology and digital services companies, for instance, often have high profit margins due to their scalable business models, making them potential candidates for lucrative dividend payouts.

However, the digital era has also disrupted several traditional industries, which have been mainstays of dividend investing. Sectors like retail, media, and transportation have all felt the heat of digital disruption, which could affect their ability to pay consistent dividends.

As we move forward, investors will need to be increasingly discerning in their stock selection, keeping a keen eye on the ways in which digitisation is affecting different industries and the companies within them. While the digital revolution may lead to some companies reducing or eliminating their dividends, it may also provide opportunities for others to start paying dividends or increase their existing ones.

The Impact of Changing Demographics

Demographics play a crucial role in economic trends, and hence in investment returns. The UK, like many other developed nations, is facing a significant demographic shift with an ageing population.

This ageing demographic presents both challenges and opportunities for dividend investors. On the challenge side, ageing populations can lead to slower economic growth, which might affect companies' profitability and their ability to pay dividends.

On the opportunity side, industries that cater to older populations, such as healthcare, pharmaceuticals, and certain consumer goods, could see increased demand, potentially boosting their profits and dividends.

The Imperative of Environmental Considerations

Environmental concerns have become increasingly prominent in recent years, giving rise to a more conscious form of capitalism. Many companies, in response to investor and consumer demand, are taking steps to reduce their environmental footprint and contribute to sustainability.

In this transition to a greener economy, some sectors stand to gain more than others. Renewable energy companies, for instance, could potentially become significant dividend payers in the future. However, industries such as fossil fuels, which have been traditional sources of dividends but are now under environmental scrutiny, may face challenges.

This is not to say that all companies in these sectors will cease to be good dividend payers. Some may successfully adapt to a low-carbon economy and continue to generate profits and pay dividends. The key for the dividend investor is to closely monitor these transitions and be ready to adjust their portfolio accordingly.

Globalisation and Political Factors

Globalisation has brought about increased intercon- nectivity and interdependence among the world's economies. This has implications for UK dividend investors, as global economic trends and events can affect UK companies' earnings and, hence, their dividend payouts.

Furthermore, political factors, both domestic and international, can impact dividend investing. Changes in tax laws, regulatory policies, and trade agreements, to name a few, can affect companies' profitability and their ability to distribute dividends.

The ongoing uncertainties around Brexit exemplify this interplay of globalisation and politics. The final outcome and its implications for various sectors of the UK economy could have a significant impact on future dividends.

The key takeaway here is that the future of dividend investing in the UK, as with any form of investing, will be influenced by a multitude of factors that are often beyond our control. But rather than viewing these changes and uncertainties as threats, we should see them as opportunities for learning, adaptation, and growth.

As we embark on this journey towards the future, let us not forget the core principles that have served us well so far. Patience, consistency, diversification, and a keen eye for quality remain as relevant in the future as they are today. And while it's essential to keep an eye on the horizon and anticipate changes, it's equally important to stay grounded in the fundamentals.

The future might be uncertain, but armed with the right mindset, sound strategies, and a thirst for knowledge, we can confidently sail towards it, seizing the opportunities that come our way and steering clear of potential pitfalls. In this manner, we can ensure that dividend investing continues to be a rewarding journey for us, just as it has been for countless investors who have tread this path before us.

In closing, dividend investing is not just about the money. It's about financial independence, about building a safety net for your family, about securing a comfortable retirement, and, perhaps most importantly, about the peace of mind that comes from knowing you're well-prepared for whatever the future might hold.

Keep learning, keep investing, and keep reaping the rewards of your patience and wisdom. Here's to a future filled with dividends!

Our Thanks and A Request

Firstly, we would like to extend our heartfelt appreciation to you, our esteemed reader. Your commitment to enriching your understanding of dividend investing, and your decision to embark on this enlightening journey with us, is the reason why we created this guide.

We sincerely hope that "Dividend Investing for Beginners: A Simple, Succinct & Comprehensive Guide to Dividend Investing for UK Investors" has provided you with valuable insights, strategies, and tools that will bolster your dividend investing journey.

Having reached this stage, it's safe to say that you are no longer a novice in the realm of dividend investing. We trust that the knowledge you've gleaned from these pages will equip you with the confidence to make informed decisions, reduce risks, and ultimately, reap the rewards of your carefully chosen investments.

Your Experience Matters to Us

In this fast-paced world of digital publishing, feedback from readers like you is the cornerstone of our growth and improvement. It helps us understand what resonates with our readers, what we are doing right, and perhaps most importantly, areas where we could provide even more value.

Help Us Reach More Aspiring Investors

If you found this book helpful and think it might benefit others, we kindly request you to leave a review on Amazon. Your review will not only help us understand your perspective, but it will also enable us to reach more individuals who are venturing into the world of dividend investing.

Whether you choose to provide a star rating, a brief note, or a detailed review, each contribution helps. Your valuable input will guide potential readers to make an informed decision, while at the same time, it fuels our commitment to provide even better content in the future.

Thank You for Your Support

Once again, thank you for your time, your trust, and your commitment to financial growth. Remember, the journey of investing is a long-term endeavour filled with opportunities for learning and growth. We hope that this guide has prepared you for the first steps of this rewarding adventure.

So, here's to your journey in dividend investing. May your dividends be plentiful, and your financial future, prosperous.

We are eager to hear about your experiences. To leave a review, simply go to the Amazon page where you purchased this book, scroll down to the customer reviews, and click on 'Write a customer review.' Thank you again for your support.

Remember, your journey doesn't end here. Continue learning, continue investing, and continue growing. Here's to your financial success!